I GO THERE WITH YOU

THE U2 SITES
OF SOUTHERN CALIFORNIA,
FROM SIGNIFICANT
TO SACRED

BROOK W. FLAGG

◯NINE CRITERIA PRESS

I GO THERE WITH YOU:
The U2 Sites of Southern California,
From Significant To Sacred

Contact: brookwf@gmail.com
Front cover design: Brook W. Flagg
Back cover design: Brook W. Flagg
Interior collage artwork: Brook W. Flagg
Licensed photo copyrights and contributor photo credits are in text.

ISBN: 9798265819598
First Edition: October 2025

10 9 8 7 6 5 4 3 2 1
Printed in the United States of America.

To Chris
AIWIY

To the U2 community
I hope this book is useful.

To U2
Thanks for giving us a great life.

To myself
May I be happy. May I be healthy.
May I be free from suffering.

CONTENTS

Introduction

"It is worth mentioning that more people live off their imaginations in California than any other place in the world. No other geography comes close."[1]

– Bono, Palm Springs Film Festival, January 4, 2014

From Significant to Sacred

There are stretches of land throughout Southern California where music and the mystical intersect. Countless musical artists have notoriously drawn inspiration from these vortexes; among them is the band U2, which formed 5,000 miles away in another fabled land, the nation of Ireland, on September 25, 1976.

When the musical aspirations of Dublin schoolmates Paul Hewson (Bono), David Evans (The Edge), and Adam Clayton led them to the home of younger student Larry Mullen Jr.— who had pinned a note on the bulletin board of Mount Temple Comprehensive School advertising his intentions to form a band— not one of them had been to California. In fact, only The Edge had visited the United States at all.

But within a few short years, U2 would arrive in Southern California for the first time—together as a band of brothers, but each one a stranger in a strange land. Over the decades, they would return again and again to find a backdrop for their lyrics, a playground for men clinging to boyish spirits, and spaces that mirrored their perpetual search for meaning. This book is about that search. It's about the golden days when "a band from the north side of Dublin" explored the south side of California's furthest reaches, filled with moments that accompanied them from innocence to experience.

Some of these sites remain quiet corners of the Golden State that still hum with the energy of the band's presence; they are sacred, hallowed grounds that played essential roles in specific chapters of U2's story. This book refers to them as Sacred Sites. Other places are simpler, yet significant enough to be stops along

---

1   "U2News - Sonny Bono Visionary Award 2014." Ezequiel EspañOl. January 4, 2014. Video, https://www.youtube.com/watch?v=YHitTokwedI.

the way—fun destinations where fans can go to say, "U2 was here, and so was I." This book refers to them as Sites of Significance. Although most of the locations and establishments included are still in operation and visitable, some are not. This book aims to make the present condition of each site clear, along with a distinction that gets straight to the point on what makes each site significant in U2 history.

Every Site Has a Story

For those who have followed U2 across decades and continents, this book presents the possibility of multiple journeys. It can be an essential companion when planning a pilgrimage to the Southern California sites where the band once found inspiration or made an impact.

Each site we explore, from a golden beach to a desert badland to an urban intersection, tells a unique story. Each one is part of a moment in time that can never be repeated—but it *can* be revisited, and that is my intention as the author. To support your journey, I have gathered facts through documented U2 history, plus reflections shared by the band members, their associates, the journalists who covered U2's presence in the region, and fans who were the original storytellers. Moreover, through scrapbooked personal reflections and photographs from myself and fellow travelers, this book invites you to see Southern California through the lens of seekers who embrace U2's music as spiritual sustenance—and perhaps more importantly, to feel what it means to chase something bigger than yourself across the endless horizon with no line. It's about music as a compass, experience as a teacher, and landscape as an inspiration, all of which have been masterfully captured in U2's lyrics for nearly fifty years.

From the Beginning

Although *The Joshua Tree* is perhaps the best-known example of U2's artistic immersion in California, the journey neither begins nor ends there. U2 first arrived in California in 1981, just five years after forming the band and a few months after the release of their debut album, *Boy*. The region is both sacred and significant to the lore and legacy of four Irish pilgrims and their fans—and the journey continues to unfold, with new generations stepping into the dust trails left behind. Whether you've been a fan for five decades or five days—and whether you're actively planning a U2-inspired road trip or simply dreaming of one—this is your invitation to trace the lines of an invisible map and begin plotting your own journey.

Because in the end, the beauty of these places isn't just that U2 was there. It's that you can be there, too...and through this book, I go there with you.

Love and Peace,
Brook (the author)

SECTION I

Early Sites of Significance

Reseda Country Club

> **Location:** 18419 Sherman Way, Reseda
>
> **Significance:** First California performance; first *Los Angeles Times* review
>
> **Date in U2 history:** March 15, 1981
>
> **Still in operation/visitable?** No
>
> **Building still standing?** Yes

"The first show we ever played in LA was at the Country Club, a 1,200-seater in the Valley. It sold out because we had radio support in advance."[2]

– Original U2 manager Paul McGuiness, *Billboard*, 2014

Touring for their debut album, *Boy*, was a demanding regimen for a young U2. As the two oldest members of the band, Adam Clayton and Bono were twenty years old when the European leg kicked off in September 1980. The Edge (who will be referred to only as "Edge" for the remainder of this book) had turned nineteen the month prior, and Larry Mullen Jr. was eighteen until almost two months into the tour. Before the *Boy* tour, the band's only experience playing outside of Ireland was a two-week sprint of twelve shows in December 1979, when they stopped at various cities throughout England to promote the *U2-3* EP. A mere nine months later, they would embark on an aggressive international tour schedule for their first full-length record.

After fifty-seven European shows, the band headed to North America for the second leg. As documented in the "City of Blinding Lights" lyrics, playing their first American show in New York City mesmerized the wide-eyed foursome in a way that other Irish and British bands of the era were not willing to indulge. U2 rejected the cynicism that held back the legion of "English fashion bands passing

---

2   Waddell, Ray. "Billboard's 2014 Industry Icon: Paul McGuinness on 35 Years Guiding 'The Biggest Band in the World' (Q&A)." *Billboard*, January 17, 2014.

through," a virtue that was to their benefit. In the book *U2: Songs + Experience*, Niall Stokes wrote, "U2 crossed the Atlantic knowing that they had a lot to learn, conscious that they needed to establish a foundation there in order to further their ambition to become the biggest rock band in the world. Their first trip to New York was a magical experience, and one they'd never forget."[3]

The band's U.S. debut at The Ritz took place on December 6. There was a stretch of ten shows along the East Coast, followed by a third leg that returned them to Europe through the holiday season, over the new year, and into February. The fourth leg of the tour put them back in the States to cycle through the East Coast once again. It was strategically designed to coincide with the U.S. release of *Boy* on March 3, 1981.

Then, after shuffling between both continents for six months and 103 shows, U2 finally arrived on the West Coast to play in California for the first time. This is where we find the first Southern California site of significance for the band, in an unlikely suburban enclave of the San Fernando Valley. The date was March 15, 1981. The venue was Wolf and Rissmiller's Country Club in Reseda. And the rest was history.

Not That Kind of Country Club

People remember the establishment by a profusion of names; in addition to Wolf and Rissmiller's, it has been called the Reseda Country Club, Chuck Landis' Country Club, and simply the Country Club. In truth, the venue operated under a somewhat misleading DBA; Wolf and Rissmiller's was not the kind of country club to offer tennis lessons or tee times.

Instead, the hall on Sherman Way near Reseda Boulevard was given its name by the Roxy Theatre's co-founder Chuck Landis in 1980 to signify that the majority of those booked to play there were, in fact, country music acts.[4] A March 1980 Los Angeles Public Library photo of the marquee prior to the club's grand opening

---

3   Stokes, Niall, and Brian Boyd. 2018. *U2: Songs + Experience*. Carlton Books.

4   Quinn, James. "Chuck Landis, Veteran Concert Promoter, Dies at Home at 68." *Los Angeles Times*, March 10, 1986.

reveals that its first performers were country artists Merle Haggard, Tanya Tucker, and Donna Fargo.[5]

One year later, under the management of promoter Jim Rissmiller and his business partner Steve Wolf, the Country Club would broaden its appeal by booking everyone from B.B. King, to Iggy Pop, to Mötley Crüe. By '85, the venue would go full metal by hosting bands like Slayer. Before that, a steady stream of punk and new wave acts passed through the Country Club—and in March '81, one such act was U2.

In his memoir *Surrender: 40 Songs, One Story*, Bono wrote the following reflection: "Our first show was at the Reseda Country Club with six hundred people, one of whom was the *LA Times* critic Robert Hilburn, a genius of compression known for terse, melodrama-free analysis. The band ... couldn't have asked for a better welcome to the country/Country Club, and his rave review that appeared on the front page of the Calendar section."[6]

Hilburn's review includes the observation: "... the band with the most commercial potential here may be U2, a gutty and richly talented young Irish quartet which made its local debut Sunday night at the Country Club in Reseda ... Gradually, the economy and intelligence of the music, coupled with the purity and heart of Hewson's vocals, broke down the audience's reserve."[7]

Boy, Stupid Boy

Multiple audio recordings of the full Reseda Country Club show exist, both online and on a decades-old bootleg called "U2 The Ides of March" (alternated with the name "U2 the *Ideas* of March" on its packaging). In the audio, some highlights that can be heard from Bono include:

- The classic Bonoism, "We're not just another English band passing through. First of all, we're Irish."

---

5   "Chuck Landis' Country Club." TESSA: Digital Collections of the Los Angeles Public Library. Digital Public Library of America, August 13, 2025.

6   Bono. 2022. *Surrender: 40 Songs, One Story*. Penguin Random House.

7   "1981-03-15 Country Club, Reseda, CA, USA." U2songs.Com. https://www.u2songs.com/shows/1981_03_15_u2_country_club_reseda_california.

- Added to this was, "And we plan to stay here a little while—three months, actually. And we're gonna knock on people's doors, maybe the radio, until they let us in, until they let *you* in."
- After the instrumental "Things to Make and Do," Bono informed the crowd, "In Ireland … the seats at a place, they're called cabaret." This prompted a heckler to shout, "What part of Ireland are you from, huh?!" To this, Bono retorted, "There's some more people from Ireland, is that right? We're always loud, anyway."
- Another attendee can be heard telling the heckler to shut up. After introducing "Stories for Boys," Bono concluded the interaction with, "We'd very much like if you could give to us, then we'd give more back to you." He then shouted what could be audibly interpreted as either, "Make up your own mind!" or "Think of your own life!"[8]
- In the audio, Bono is never heard addressing the crowd that night as "Los Angeles," "California," or any other location. As U2's touring career progressed, acknowledging locations would become an expected element of every show.

"The Next Thing You Know, We're Out of Control"

Although the U2 camp has generally spoken of "I Will Follow" as the band's first successful single in the U.S.—and, has often thanked KROQ FM for being one the first American radio stations to play it—the Reseda Country Club recording reveals that some audience members shouted requests for "Out of Control" immediately after "Another Time, Another Place," indicating that *Boy*'s first single may have gained more traction in the U.S. than the band was aware.

Despite these audience pleas, there was no deviation from the common set. They played "The Cry/The Electric Co." next as planned, with "Out of Control" as the main set finale. Some cheering and synchronized clapping can be heard when it begins.

Twenty years later on November 12, 2001—on the third leg of the *Elevation* tour, at the band's first night playing the Los Angeles venue then known as the Staples Center—"Out of Control" was the song Bono chose to bookend his reference to the *Boy* tour and Reseda Country Club show.

---

8   1981 03 15 Los Angeles, California Reseda Country Club." Adrian Newman. March 13, 2019. Video, YouTube.

During the song's instrumental bridge, a section that is often used as a device for him to introduce the band or share early U2 memories of the city in which U2 is performing, Bono recalled, "We go from London to New York, from New York to Los Angeles ... Reseda, where we saw the Country Club. Woke up the next morning, and on the front of the Calendar section is a picture of our band. The critic Robert Hilburn says we're gonna get there in the end. And we believed him! The next thing you know, we're out of control!"[9]

What Happened to the Country Club?

Although the original building at 18419 Sherman Way is still standing as of 2025, the facility is now operating as a church. The Country Club closed as a music venue in 2000.

In 2012, an *LA Weekly* retrospective by Bailey Pennick included this update: "Restauracion Reseda has taken over the Country Club; the large leather booths and bar are gone, replaced by video screens for projected hymn lyrics and a simple stage for the choir and pastor. Rest assured that the acoustics are still excellent."[10]

Ready for What's Next

Throughout the well-connected circles of club promoters who propelled the music scenes of various LA suburbs in the early 80s, U2's Reseda Country Club show triggered fast-spreading buzz about the new band from Ireland. Having conquered Los Angeles as they saw it—made complete by Robert Hilburn's supportive *LA Times* review—U2 was ready for what was next. One day later, the band would travel sixty miles southeast for their next Southern California conquest: Orange County.

9   "U2 - 2001-11-12 - Los Angeles, California - Staples Center (Full Show)." U2start. April 22, 2020. Video, YouTube.

10 Pennick, Bailey. "What Happened to the Reseda Country Club?" *LA Weekly*, October 16, 2012. https://www.laweekly.com/what-happened-to-the-reseda-country-club/.

Woodstock Concert Theatre

Location: 951 S. Knott Ave., Anaheim
Significance: First Orange County performance; crowd size mystery; only known full band trip to Disneyland
Date in U2 history: March 16, 1981
Still in operation/visitable? No
Building still standing? No

"Far and away the most intriguing new band to pop up in the last six months is an Irish group called U2."[11]

– C.P. Smith, *Orange County Register*, 1981

The day after their first California performance in Reseda, U2 headed to Orange County to play a pizza parlor turned all-ages venue in Anaheim called the Woodstock Concert Theatre.

Owned by the Schultz family and managed by its patriarch Joseph "Old Boy" Schultz, the Woodstock was, at first, a club frequented exclusively by young metalheads. Although most of the bands who came through would eventually fizzle out, a handful found success in the years that followed. Case in point: On October 22, 1982, the Woodstock hosted a show featuring four metal acts; the lowest billing went to one called Metallica, and you've likely never heard of the other three.

But before any of those bands played the Woodstock, a decidedly un-metal foursome from Ireland had already descended on Schultz's club the previous year. The night was March 16, 1981, when U2 played for a crowd that—depending on who you ask—could have been less than a dozen, or close to one hundred.

---

11 Carpenter, Eric. "Mr. Anaheim: Keeping Tabs on U2 from Anaheim's Woodstock Club to the Forum." *Orange County Register*, June 8, 2015. https://www.ocregister.com/2015/06/08/mr-anaheim-keeping-tabs-on-u2-from-anaheims-woodstock-club-to-the-forum/.

Gang of Youths

Mike Muckenthaler was part of a tight-knit group of teens and twenty-somethings who were friends of Old Boy's three sons and worked for the Woodstock in its heyday. He is among a small number of attendees who provided their recollections of the show to the author. In March '81, Muckenthaler's responsibilities ranged from booking the acts to promoting the shows to erranding for the bands.

Although the Ramones played there in November '79, the Woodstock was still better known as a venue for metal acts rather than punk; Muckenthaler was aiming to change that. "I was the guy pushing for more diversity in the acts they booked," he said. "I had brought in Social Distortion to do a show earlier, and there was a minor riot between our security, the band, and their fans." Despite that hiccup, "We were kind of giving new wave and punk a second try with U2."

Other than the obvious—"Direct from Ireland," said the flyer— the Woodstock gang didn't know much about U2 at the time. "We seriously thought they were going to be a Flock of Seagulls type band," Muckenthaler recalled. The kids were in for a surprise; in fact, Muckenthaler remembers comparing what he saw that night to a performance by one of the most legendary Los Angeles bands of all time. "I'd seen The Doors play at a local college when I was still in high school," he said. "And that night, I had the same feeling that something magical was happening with *this* band, something original and inspirational. We were blown away by what we heard that night."

When the young Woodstock staff would interact with the bands they booked, their experiences were typically more grit than glamour; U2, it turned out, was no exception. "I had to go home and get an iron so Bono's shirt would look good," Muckenthaler recalled, "because they didn't have any clothes that weren't wrinkled. Can you imagine, ironing Bono's shirt and thinking, 'I hope this is going to be worth it.'" He returned with his mother's iron to press the white blouse into perfection. Although there are no published photos of the Woodstock gig, many *Boy*-era photos show that Bono's unofficial uniform for the tour included a white, crisply starched button-down.

The Attendance Mystery

As stated, there are varying accounts of how many people were in the club that night. Some say there were eleven; others say there were one hundred. In U2's nearly five decades of live performance, it may be the largest attendance discrepancy on record. It turns out that the source of the mystery is quintessential of the era: the venue's casual admittance policy. Muckenthaler, who made the Woodstock's promotional materials, said that showing up to the club with a flyer would commonly substitute for holding a traditional ticket. Often, the bands were paid according to how many people showed up with the flyer in hand. He surmised that this accounted for the attendance discrepancy.

"There were two other bands there that night," he said, "one of which had a party bus with their fans in it." Both bands (called Second Wind and The Radiomusic, respectively) had flyers and presale tickets of their own. Although U2 got paid upfront, said Muckenthaler, "Only eleven or twelve actual customers bought tickets that night that weren't there for the other two bands. So, U2 [only] got credit for those customers."

Other firsthand accounts are aligned with this theory. In the review section of the show's entry in the U2Gigs.com database, attendee LeRoy A. Lucian wrote, "There may have only been a dozen or so in attendance who came just for the band, but there were about one hundred or so in the club that night."[12]

In short, the attendance mystery of U2's second California show boils down to who was there for *them* versus who was just ... there. By the time U2 took the stage, the club had mostly cleared out. "The band with the party bus loaded up after their set and left," Muckenthaler said. This resulted in about a dozen people remaining in the room.

Attendance mystery solved.

---

12   LeRoy, Lucian A. U2gigs.com. https://www.u2gigs.com/show171.html.

An 80s Aura

Lucian's recollection of the evening captures its early 80s aura. "There were the slam dancers near the stage, the black leather and mascara guys who mostly hung near the bar, and a veritable cornucopia of strangely attired humanity filling the voids," he wrote. "From the obligatory tall mohawks to this one girl with a swirl of white hair dyed pink on top that looked like a lit stick match ... One young, long-haired guy was dancing away with an old tape recorder on his shoulder. At one point, this young couple walked through the door looking like they came straight from a school dance. She was wearing a prom-type dress and he was wearing a blazer with a crest on the pocket. They took two steps in and stayed by the door all night, but they stayed. The sights before them must have been quite a culture shock."

Michael Marsh was also in attendance that night, after being turned on to U2's debut record two months before its American release. "I was working at Anaheim Tower Records and got a promo copy of *Boy* in January," he said. "Some friends heard about the gig, and we were expecting something special. We showed up in the afternoon to see them arrive off the bus for the soundcheck. I still wonder how or why we did that." He recalled that tickets were $5.50, a price that was too much for one friend who decided to pass—especially because "we were eighteen and nineteen and couldn't get a beer."

Regarding the set, Marsh said, "The band had barely enough songs for a set, and they played '11 O'Clock Tick Tock' a second time as an encore." Repeating "11 O'Clock Tick Tock" after the main set was a device employed throughout the *Boy* tour, including the previous night in Reseda. It didn't seem to hurt, at least not in Anaheim. "It was the eve of St. Patrick's Day and they were totally on fire," Marsh said. "Everybody knows them now, but at the time, we seriously thought we'd seen the best band ever. They weren't pompous, corny, or lame like so many of the bands of that time. They were uniquely optimistic and sincere."

C.P. Smith, then the *Orange County Register* rock critic, was among the crowd. He wrote in his review: *"The music sounded so natural and 'right' that one felt as though it had always been there, like gold nuggets lying around waiting to be discovered ... U2's music is like this. It's also an almost indescribable mixture of various facets of rock and pop. And maybe it's better that the group's songs can't be fully explained ... [they are] attractively melodic, yet maintain the hard edge of rock that makes the group a strong live show."* [13]

Nothing for U2 Play

No video or audio recordings of the Woodstock show exist online. Those who frequented the club surmise that Old Boy Schultz would film most performances, attempt to sell the tapes to the bands, and recycle the unsold tapes by filming over them. In a Facebook group devoted to maintaining the Woodstock's legacy, it has been speculated that the U2 show was among the recycled. No official setlist has ever been published; a logical assumption is that the common *Boy* tour setlist was played.

Meanwhile, the owner of a different Orange County club never lived down the decision to pass on letting four kids from Ireland play *his* venue that year. "I talked to Jerry Roach about it once," Muckenthaler recalled. "Jerry owned the Cuckoo's Nest club in Costa Mesa, a famous punk venue. He said no [to U2], and he told me that it was the only show he regretted not booking. All these years later, it still bothered him."

Getting Lost with Mickey Mouse

The day after the Woodstock show, the members of U2 reportedly took a trip to Disneyland. It may be the only time all four visited The Happiest Place on Earth™ together, along with manager Paul McGuinness, before they each started their respective families. There are no photos of the trip online; while compiling information for this book, an attempt was made to source any photos that may exist. It was shared by anonymous anecdote that one young member of the Woodstock group accompanied the band to the park; according to her friends who reminisce about the Woodstock legacy

13   Carpenter, Eric. "Mr. Anaheim: Keeping Tabs on U2 from Anaheim's Woodstock Club to the Forum." *Orange County Register*, June 8, 2015. https://www.ocregister.com/2015/06/08/mr-anaheim-keeping-tabs-on-u2-from-anaheims-woodstock-club-to-the-forum/.

online, she is deceased. It was said that "she would be the only one who would have photos."

Amid the unfortunate absence of photo documentation, the strongest evidence that a U2 Disneyland trip took place that week in March 1981 was a comment from Bono himself, made twenty-four years later when the *Vertigo* tour arrived in Anaheim. He made it at a point in the set that immediately preceded the performance of four *Boy* tracks ("The Cry," "The Electric Co.," "An Cat Dubh," and "Into the Heart"). Throughout the *Vertigo* tour, Bono would use that point in the set to briefly reflect on the band's *Boy* tour stop in that city or region. The night of April 2, 2005, he told the crowd at the Honda Center (then known as the Arrowhead Pond of Anaheim), "We came here a long time ago, when we were playing the clubs, getting lost with Mickey Mouse and Donald Duck at Disneyland, four boys from Ireland, playing this tune."[14]

It's not a photo, but it's a confirmation.

The "Biggest Regret"

The Woodstock Concert Theatre is long gone; it operated for five years and closed in 1984. The Knott Avenue address is now a vacant lot, but the venue lives on in U2 history as the indisputable site of the band's first Orange County performance.

Muckenthaler, who saw many now-infamous bands in the Woodstock's most active years, has crystallized the impression U2 made on him that night in 1981. "U2 was a band no one could pigeonhole or define in any narrow terms," he said. "All of us there knew this was something special. Our biggest regret is that we didn't know enough to really promote them. Our metal kids didn't come to the show, and the punks didn't know what U2 was all about. Maybe that's why they're still around; originality and creativity are something that inspires the soul. It did that night and it still does now."

14 "U2 2005-04-02 Anaheim, Arrowhead Pond - Full Show - JAM/Slickmode Master Tape Collection." Ryan J. September 9, 2024. Video, https://www.youtube.com/watch?v=niD8Pe4gNbY.

No Orange County Confusion

Many artists from outside the U.S. have notoriously struggled to grasp the distinction between Orange County and LA; U2 is not among them. On April 24, 2001, Bono would tell the *Elevation* crowd at the Arrowhead Pond, "It's a great night to be in U2, and a great night to be in Anaheim."[15] During the seventh leg of *U2 360°* on June 17, 2011, he would emerge onstage at Angels Stadium opening with "Even Better Than the Real Thing." As he instructed fans to lift their arms for the bridge of the song, Bono invoked the name of the Major League Baseball team: "Angels, where you gonna take us tonight? You take us higher!"[16]

15   "U2 - 2001-04-24 - Anaheim, California - Arrowhead Pond (Full Show)." U2Start. April 23, 2020. Video, YouTube.

16   "U2 360 Tour Live Full Concert Show Multicam Anaheim California June 18 2011 Soundboard IEM Audio USA." Jovi Neri. November 20, 2022. Video, YouTube.

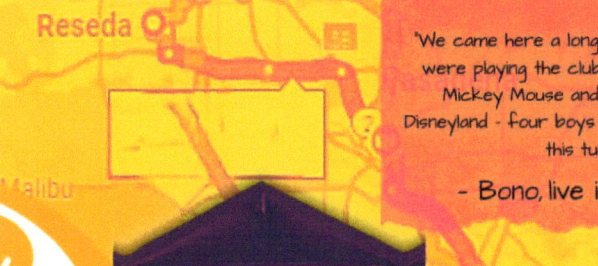

"We came here a long time ago, when we were playing the clubs, getting lost with Mickey Mouse and Donald Duck at Disneyland - four boys from Ireland, playing this tune."

- Bono, live in Anaheim | April 2, 2005

WOODSTOCK
Concert Theatre

U2
DIRECT FROM IRELAND

PLUS

RADI⊙MUSIC

Featuring Ex. 20/20 MIKE GALLO

Special Guest:

SECOND WIND

NO AGE LIMIT

info: 761-9840

MONDAY MARCH 16

KNOTT AVE.

91 FRWY.

BALL RD.

valley view

★DOORS OPEN 8:00
★ADMISSION $300
★CORNER OF KNOTT & BALL

Rock N Roll
951 S. KNOTT AVE.

WOODSTOCK
Concert Theatre
591 N. KNOTT AVE., ANAHEIM
CORNER OF BALL RD. & KNOTT AVE.

Tonight
Starstruck
Voyeur
Xeron

Monday 3/16
Only Orange County Appearances

U2
with
Second Wind
The Radio Music

Tuesday 3/17
Bad Boys
Gizmoz
Swan

PLUS SPECIAL GUEST
RENDEZVOUS
NOV. 6

Friday 3/20
Trans Axe
Miraj
Direct Drive
714/761-9840

Saturday 3/21
Suburbia
Arion's Lyre
The Light
Panic

Sunday 3/22
Totty
White Rose
Stage Fright

Tickets for
U2 and
NAUGHTY SWEETIES
ON SALE AT TICKETRON
AND AT
WOODSTOCK

Santa Monica Civic Auditorium

Location: 1855 Main Street, Santa Monica

Significance: First auditorium in California; one of two Santa Monica performances in U2 history

Date in U2 history: May 13, 1981

Still in operation/visitable? No (deemed "seismically unsafe")

Building still standing? Yes

"Whenever I meet somebody in LA that says, 'Ah, yeah, I remember seeing them in the Whiskey or the Troubadour,' I say, 'Well, actually, you didn't. We never played any of those places.' The first was the Country Club and the second show was the Santa Monica Civic, and that was in the course of the first tour."[17]

– Paul McGuinness, *Billboard*, 2014

Two months after their Southern California debut at the Reseda Country Club, U2 returned to LA on May 13, 1981 to play the 3,000-seat Santa Monica Civic Auditorium. The building, highly recognizable for the glass curtain and brise soleil wall on its exterior front, was designed in 1958 by Louis Naidorf, architect of the iconic Capitol Records building. At the time, it was the second-largest auditorium in the Los Angeles area.

The event the Santa Monica Civic is best known for is the Teenage Awards Music International (T.A.M.I.) show in October 1964 featuring the likes of The Beach Boys, Chuck Berry, James Brown, Marvin Gaye, Smokey Robinson & the Miracles, The Supremes, and a very young The Rolling Stones. Seventeen years later, the venue would host U2.

17 Waddell, Ray. "Special Feature: Paul McGuinness Reflects on 35 Years as Mentor in Chief for U2." *Billboard*, December 31, 2014. https://www.billboard.com/music/music-news/special-feature-paul-mcguinness-reflects-on-35-years-as-mentor-in-chief-5877961/.

The "I Will Follow" Effect

When speaking to *Billboard* in 2014, McGuinness recalled how the band managed to circle back to LA so quickly on the *Boy* tour. "The first (in LA) was the Country Club, and the second show was the Santa Monica Civic, and that was in the course of the first tour. LA was always a very strong market for us ... because of good promoters."[18]

The record had been on shelves for seven months at that point, but only two months in the U.S. Once the airplay of "I Will Follow" on KROQ-FM reached saturation, exposure on other stations soon followed. In his *Surrender* memoir, Bono wrote about the phenomenon: *"Edge and I were stopped at some lights in Los Angeles and noticed 'I Will Follow' being played on a radio station in a car to our right. And also being played on another station, in a car to our left. Beautifully out of sync. The boy was sprinting. We had to keep up."*[19]

Not Catching Cat Scratch Fever

Once again, Wolf & Rissmiller was the promoter; the venue (and the higher attendance that came with it) were the main distinguishing characteristics from the club shows that preceded. The show took place on a Wednesday, a school night for many younger attendees.

To a lesser extent, the date is remembered for Bono's rant about Ted Nugent, whose show the band caught the night before at the Los Angeles Sports Arena (two years later, U2 would play their own first headlining arena show there). An online anecdote of Bono's monologue about the experience appears on U2gigs.com: *"So, we saw a Ted Nugent show recently. I took some notes."* (Looks at a paper in hand). *"Ted said a few things. It might be because we're Irish, but I don't completely understand this. Maybe you can tell me what this means ... Alright, alright, alright, alright alright, alright."*[20]

An entry for the show on U2songs.com provides some additional context: *In addition, the show follows a night where Bono*

---

18 Waddell, Ray. "Billboard's 2014 Industry Icon: Paul McGuinness on 35 Years Guiding 'The Biggest Band in the World' (Q&A)." *Billboard*, January 17, 2024. https://www.billboard.com/music/music-news/billboards-2014-industry-icon-paul-mcguinness-on-35-5876780/.

19 Bono. 2022. *Surrender: 40 Songs, One Story*. Penguin Random House.

20 Bruce. "U2 From 5 Feet Away." U2gigs.Com. Accessed August 23, 2025. https://www.u2gigs.com/show365.html.

went and saw Ted Nugent perform at the Sports Arena, and during the show Bono mimics Nugent's stage behavior, joking with the audience about all the rock and roll clichés that were present the night before in the show Bono had witnessed. "Thank you, Los Angeles, you're the greatest!" and other clichés are read from a paper Bono brought with him to the show.[21]

Today, the idea of any member of U2 taking in a Ted Nugent show seems utterly foreign. But indeed, it is verifiable that Nugent played the Los Angeles Sports Arena on May 12, 1981 on his *Scream Dream* tour.

"Boyishly and Gallantly...Vibrant and Real"

A review of U2 and opening act The Suburban Lawns (a Long Beach-based band best known for their song "Gidget Goes to Hell") was written by an assortment of contributors for the publication *Data-Boy*, a magazine that circulated throughout the West Hollywood gay scene for decades—and, for a time, covered the burgeoning punk scene with reviews of early-80s shows by X, The Go-Go's, Missing Persons, and David Bowie.

The primary reviewer was Judy Zee of Venice Beach, described as "the last hippie in SoCal." What follows is her May '81 review of U2 in Santa Monica, archived on TVParty.com:

— *And now some variegated viewpoints from the venerable Judy Zee, who's (sic) article was bumped from last issue. She covers the incredible U2 show at the Santa Monica Civic a few weeks ago. Eye also attended and enjoyed the show, it was incredible to see a band with so much power and presence. Judy writes here with her partner Punkasso who, you may remember, made clear his dislike of U2 in a previous column.*

U2's got lust for life! by — PZ Connection

U2's music is so vibrant and real, they send rushes out into the audience, they are alive and perform with gusto. They give fully of themselves. They have a lot to offer. Too bad they couldn't be seen by half the people here.

---

21 "1981-05-13 Santa Monica Civic Auditorium , Santa Monica, CA." https://www.u2songs.com/shows/1981_05_13_u2_santa_monica_civic_auditorium__santa_monica_california.

The ticketholders at the back of the Santa Monica Civic were moving and dancing despite the fact that they couldn't see the band. Bono boyishly and gallantly bounded up the amplifier stack to the top, carrying with him a big ol' American flag.

The spotlights followed this charade, for all to see a distinct drop of the flag into an abrupt darkness as he was helped off by his stage manager (who nearly dropped him, cute buns and all!).

The Zee found this adorable Irish boy's action a rather funny stunt. 'America' it symbolized, but Amerika what?!? This country right now is in such an awful state, the gesture appeared quite laughably pathetic.

Punkasso looked at this action from an interestingly different angle, perhaps he was simulating the outcry of U2's home land for a strong, authoritative leader, such as our president who can survive three bullet holes in the chest and not worry about starving because he eats on a government pension plan, rather than the weak rationality of the recent loss of England's starving fanatical prisoner of war, Bobby Sands, who justified the irregularity of a small disorganized country in turmoil, grasping at straws.

Musically U2 was quite impressive, or was it the lights blending so with the sound? Anyway, Punkasso fell asleep during the show, must have been a form of psychic toxic shock, while Zee stared right into the overpowering strong white lights emitted from the stage.

This joyful boy leading the band, Captain of the sub, was clad in Irish plaid pants, contorting with Jagger-esue movements while the jiving exploring guitarist, The Edge, played melodic P.I.L. simulated riffs. The lights changed over the audience heads in strong sweeps of color. That light show was fabulous, the lights were all bouncing to an audience of mostly juvenile suburbanite non-punks, outcasts of their mother's wombs...

Take a deep breath for The Suburban Lawns who attempted to warm the audience up before U2 came on. Every time I see them, I realize they need a good fertilizer and a good cutting up (to shreds). I mean, a song about lust over a janitor's genitals? Come on now![22]

Not bad for a school night.

The First Time

This was the first of only two Santa Monica performances in U2 history. The next would be thirty-three years later on January 6, 2014, to film the video for the single "Invisible." The shoot was in the Barker Hanger, an event space at the Santa Monica Airport; around 1,200 hired extras made up the crowd for the three-day shoot. A sixty-second clip of the video aired during the Super Bowl on February 2, 2014 to launch a partnership between Bono-founded project (RED) and Bank of America, which raised $3 million for the fight against AIDS.

---

22 Zee, Judy. "U2's Got Lust for Life." *Data-Boy*, June 11, 1981. http://www.tvparty.com/homeroom1/6-11-81.html.

KROQ 106.7 AND WOLF & RISSMILLER CONCERTS BRING

"U2's music is so vibrant and real, they send rushes out into the audience, they are alive and perform with gusto. They give fully of themselves."

- Judy Zee, Data Boy

KROQ 107 & WOLF
RISSMILLER CONCERTS

U 2

TA MONICA CIVIC AU

13 1981   SANTA
WED
8:0

THIS WEDNESDAY

Special Guest

SUBURBAN LAWNS

WEDNESDAY, MAY 13 · 8PM

 Festival Style General Admission
Advance. $7.50/Day of Show, $8.50.

Tickets available at Santa Monica Civic Box Office, and Ticketron. Information and Phone Charge (213) 393-9961

PRODUCED BY WOLF & RISSMILLER CONCERTS

KROQ & WOLF & RISSMILLER
PRESENT

U2

**MAY 13
SANTA MONICA
CIVIC**

ISLAND Records & Tapes

Glen Helen Regional Park: The US Festival

Location: 2555 Glen Helen Pkwy, San Bernardino

Significance: First American festival; only American festival for more than 30 years; history-making Bono stage antics

Date in U2 history: May 30, 1983

Still in operation/visitable? Yes

"During the U.S. leg, the band played three shows that really helped to shape the course of their career going forward. The first show was U2's performance at the US Festival, their first festival performance in the States."[23]

– Melody Muraca, *Into the Heart of U2 Podcast*, 2023

Over the course of more than thirty podcast episodes recorded throughout 2023 and 2024, Melody Muraca and Bill See documented U2's legacy through the lens of two Southern California-based fans who came of age with the band and "saw it all happen in real time." The fifth episode, released on October 6, 2023, covers the *War* tour—specifically, the significance of three performances that solidified U2's American presence, two of which were in Southern California.

The U2 history canon points to one of these shows—June 5, 1983 at Red Rocks Amphitheatre in Colorado—as the starting point of the band's American revolution. This position often goes unchallenged; after all, the show colloquially known as "Red Rocks" is forever preserved on film as *Under a Blood Red Sky*. However, one could argue that U2's American breakthrough actually began six days earlier, when the band took to an outdoor stage to make a splash at the '83 US Festival.

This was not just the band's first American festival; it would, in fact, be U2's *only* American festival for the next thirty-four

---

23 Muraca, Melody. "War (Part 2)." https://Podcasts.Apple.Com/Us/Podcast/War-part- 2/ Id1706044037?I=1000630442014. Apple Podcasts, October 6, 2023.

years. The next appearance at a festival in the States would not be until *The Joshua Tree 2017* tour made a stop at Tennessee's Bonnaroo Music & Arts Festival on September 6, 2017. These facts notwithstanding, the first American festival distinction is only a portion of the case for why the US Festival performance (which clocked in at exactly one hour) deserves a far more prominent position in U2 lore than it currently holds.

If You Don't Know: The History of the US Festival

The US Festival occurred twice over two consecutive years; U2 was booked for the second and final installment of the event, which was held in the last days of May 1983 over Memorial Day weekend. The first US Festival took place the previous September over the Labor Day weekend of 1982. Both were at Glen Helen Regional Park in San Bernardino, in an area known locally as Devore. When discussing the fortieth anniversary of *War* on the Sirius XM channel U2-X Radio, Adam Clayton innocently referred to the site as "the desert"— and in a fortieth anniversary retrospective of the US Festival, *Spin* magazine declared the location "so obscure that most SoCal residents couldn't find it on a map" (this author takes exception to that, having come from San Bernardino herself.) For what it's worth, the site is on the grounds of a landscaped regional park in the largest county in the United States. Glen Helen Regional Park remains a popular destination for picnicking, camping, and day trips; ironically, it may be the most accessible site of significance in this book.

Regardless, the full *Spin* quote by writer Sean Burch points to the location as evidence of the festival's historical import: "It was big. Real fuckin' big. A record-setting 670,000 people turned out for the second and final US Festival over Memorial Day Weekend 1983 at Glen Helen Regional Park in San Bernardino, CA—a location so obscure that even most SoCal residents couldn't find it on a map even if you gave them a free ticket."[24]

Of course, US Festival tickets were *not* free; access for all three days ranged from $37.50 to $60. Although still lower than the budgetary nightmares of today's ticket equivalents, US Festival

---

24 Burch, Sean. "'It Was the '80s – Everything Was Going On': The US Festival at 40." *Spin*, May 29, 2023.

prices were still slightly at odds with the concept that Apple co-founder Steve Wozniak had dreamed up for his event: a communal music extravaganza that would contrast the "Me Generation" ideals of early 80s culture. In the documentary *US Festival 1982: The US Generation*, Wozniak is shown explaining his inspiration. "Apple stock had gone up sky high and [I] had so much money," he said. "And I just thought, 'Wow, time for a big, huge concert in the middle of nowhere,' you know? We just go out and make our own city."[25] When Wozniak invested $12.5 million to build that "city" inside Glen Helen Regional Park, he soon discovered that holding a behemoth music festival over three days—much less, one with huge acts and six-figure attendance—would require him to divorce his vision (thumbing a nose at 80s capitalism) from the mission (actually pulling off the event).

Ironically, Wozniak would need to establish a corporation—which he named UNUSON (as in "Unite Us in Song") —to execute this decidedly *anti*-corporate affair. The investment would pay off in terms of audience experience, as documented by Erik Himmelsbach-Weinstein for *Los Angeles Magazine* in 2017: "Powered by 400,000 watts, the audio was crisp and clear, and attendees could see the stage from anywhere, thanks to strategically placed video screens—an innovative concept that offered pristine viewing even during the daytime."[26]

But in the end, Wozniak lost $10 million on the first US Festival. If a second event was to be the following year, it would require even more aggressive capitalism on his part. That started with booking bigger names, despite the first year featuring several major acts of the day, including Talking Heads, the Police, Tom Petty, and the Grateful Dead. In 1982, were there bigger names than these?

25 Wozniak, Steve. The US Generation: The 1982 US Festival.
    https://tv.apple.com/us/movie/the-us-generation-the-1982-us-festival/umc.cmc.2hfcqu03ewyur0ywbn1khcesn.

26 Himmselsbach-Weinstein, Erik. "The Music Festival That Time Forgot: Inside Steve Wozniak's US Fest."
    Los Angeles Magazine, June 28, 2017.

US Festival '83: A New Model

Wozniak determined that the '83 iteration would be structured differently—divided into three consecutive days, themed by popular musical genre.

For maximum impact, each day would feature heavy-hitting headliners:

- Day one, New Wave Day (devoted to both new wave and punk), headlined by the Clash
- Day two, Heavy Metal Day, headlined by Van Halen
- Day three, Rock Day, headlined by David Bowie

Supporting these headliners would be up-and-coming acts in each genre, one of which was unhappy about where they fit into this equation. That band was U2, originally booked for day one until they successfully argued for a switch to day three. Here's how that unfolded.

Should They Stay or Should They Go

When day one headliner the Clash recognized the clandestine capitalism going on behind the scenes in Wozniak's work, their opposition to it almost derailed the second US Festival from happening at all. As the story goes, the Clash—a band that remarkably managed to maintain peak popularity in 1983 while simultaneously falling apart from within—had learned of the $25 price point for one-day tickets. This was a problem because, at some point, they were told that one-day tickets would be $17. The $8 difference reportedly infuriated the Clash members; the only thing that angered them more was the $500,000 Wozniak offered them to play the event, which paled in comparison to the $1.5 million payday Van Halen was getting.

In 2007, Wozniak told *Spin* his recollection of the drama for "Sweaty & Filthy & Crazy & Drunk," the magazine's first retrospective of the US Festival. He recalled, "The Clash was taking some sort of workingman's revolutionary stance. I met their manager the day before the show and handed him a joke slot machine that squirted water. He did not like jokes."[27] In the end,

---

27 Russell, Steven. "Sweaty & Filthy & Crazy & Drunk." *SPIN*, May 1, 2007.

the Clash agreed to perform on the sole condition that Wozniak's organizers donate $100,000 of the band's $500,000 fee to charity. They would not sign a contract until the donation was made.

U2 and the Clash

U2 has never made a secret of their admiration for the Clash; over the years, the band has repeatedly and passionately paid homage. During the *Innocence + Experience* era of 2014 through 2018, tales of early U2 lore from the band members featured the Clash as a key source of early U2 inspiration. Throughout the Las Vegas residency era that followed, the band's acknowledgment of a connection to the Clash's music continued. On September 16, 2023, when the band filmed the video for their Vegas-adjacent single "Atomic City" on Fremont Street, Bono told the crowd of assembled per diem extras and curious onlookers that the song was "a rock 'n roll 45 in the tradition of late 70s post-punk...Blondie, the Clash."[28]

This underscores the irony that in 1983, U2—just two years away from a global breakthrough at Live Aid, which would launch them headfirst into the earnest activism that is now synonymous with the band's very name in the public consciousness—could have been derailed from performing *anywhere* by the Clash, whose ideals they strongly respected. It might be unbelievable if there were no evidence. But there *is* evidence, starting with a phone call from Bono to one of the US Festival's key organizers.

The late Colorado concert promoter Barry Fey, who had been an early champion of U2 since booking them on the *Boy* tour, was instrumental in making the '83 US Festival happen. While Fey would work with U2 the following week at Red Rocks in Colorado, he was also involved in their US Festival booking in California. In 2012, Fey told the *Orange County Register* that once the band was booked, he fielded an unexpected request directly from Bono—a request that involved putting an additional degree of separation between U2 and the punk rock icons whose acclaim they aspired

---

28 "U2 Surprises Fans in Las Vegas with a Street Performance of New Song Atomic City." Up Up and Away. September 18, 2023. Video, https://www.youtube.com/watch?v=O8QCeEteaDI.

to. Fey recalled Bono being unhappy for this reason: "They were originally booked to be on the first night with the Clash."[29]

According to Fey, U2 felt that appearing on the same billing as the Clash on a day called "new wave day" would pigeonhole them into an image they weren't excited about. Given U2's longstanding claims of strong early ties to punk and post-punk, we can speculate whether they would have been more amenable to the original slot had it been called New Wave & Punk Day (and perhaps it should have been, given the full lineup for the day—*especially* the Clash). But despite continuing to benefit from airplay on KROQ, which by then was known as the voice of the burgeoning Los Angeles new wave scene, U2 had no desire to be part of the new wave movement. As Bono would say from the US Festival stage, U2 was "not just another English fashion band passing through."

Was the reluctance to appear on the same day as the Clash simply because of U2's resistance to being caught up in the fashion-conscious new wave movement—or, was Bono displeased with the Clash for pulling a hardline negotiating stunt that almost put the festival in jeopardy—and, to use modern phraseology, "messed with the money" of all the performers?

We may never know for sure. In 2012, Fey's simple reflection was, "Bono called and said [U2 would] "really rather not be on the new wave night." He recalls Bono insisting, "We'd rather be on the rock 'n' roll night." However, there is some indication that U2 knew about the Clash's demands. When Bono declared from the stage, "Nobody twisted my arm to come here. I'm here 'cause I *want* to be here," it seems logical that he was referring to a specific act who *had* required arm-twisting. Given the demands made by the Clash in exchange for playing the festival, it is a reasonable guess that he was referring to them.

In any case, Bono's request was not a problem for the festival's organizers. The Clash was being difficult, U2 wanted to distance themselves, and that was fine with Fey. "I just moved 'em," Fey shrugged. "I'd have done anything for those guys."[30]

---

29 Wener, Ben. "The Forgotten Festival: Remembering US '82 and '83 as Steve Wozniak's Dream Bash Turns 30." *The Orange County Register*, August 31, 2012.

30 Ibid.

Boy, Stupid Boy: The U2 US Festival Performance

Whether one believes that U2's American breakthrough began with the US Festival or the Red Rocks performance six days later, the eleven-song US Festival set delivers an arguably superb example of young Bono stage antics at their most delightful. The performance is also a textbook case of what Bono has frequently called "viewing my body as an inconvenience," a reference to the highly physical, improvised stage experiments that came to define his showmanship in U2's early years.[31]

The entire '83 US Festival performance lives on via YouTube, most prominently on the channel The U2 Blue Room; these are some of the highlights.

"I Threw a Brick Through a Window" | Greeting John Lennon

As they did throughout the *War* tour, the band opened with *October*'s "Gloria," which was likely to be recognized by many in the audience as it was the first U2 video to receive significant airplay on MTV in the U.S.[32] But it was Bono's stage improvisations during the next song, the *October* track "I Threw a Brick Through a Window," that truly set U2's US Festival performance apart from other stops on the *War* tour.

The spontaneity began with Bono engaging the bronze sculpture that graced the stage; officially named *Imagine*, it was the only statue of John Lennon created during the late Beatle's lifetime.[33] Steve Wozniak was one of several wealthy entrepreneurs throughout the 80s who paid for access to *Imagine*.[34] He intended to display it on the US Festival stage and commissioned its Australian artist, Brett-Livingstone Strong, to design and create the festival poster (in an exhibit on the festival grounds, Wozniak declared Strong "The Artist of The 80's"). For several years after, *Imagine* would be installed at the Grammy Awards Music Academy in

31 Wenner, Jann S. "Bono: 'I Have Come to Peace With the Zealot I Used to Be.'" *Rolling Stone*, December 27, 2017.

32 ""Gloria" - U2." U2Songs.Com. https://www.u2songs.com/discography/gloria_u2_single.

33 "Historic Statue of John Lennon for Sale." *Music Management USA*, January 3, 2010.

34 Ibid.

Los Angeles—but before that, it was a meaningful prop for Bono to repeatedly address onstage at the '83 US Festival, starting with "I Threw a Brick Through a Window." Bono's breezy, rhetorical greeting ("How you doing, John?") gives the impression that the performers were told they would be sharing the stage with a bronze sculpture of Lennon—but when asked, Bono maintained that he wasn't. In a UPI interview after the performance, Bono stated he "just saw the statue of John Lennon there" and was inspired to acknowledge it. He would do this again during the next song, "A Day Without Me."

"A Day Without Me" | "Dear Prudence" Snippet

The first single from *Boy*, "A Day Without Me," remained a regular part of the set throughout the *War* tour. It was the third song in the US Festival set, linked to "I Threw a Brick Through a Window" by drum segue (a progression that began on the *October* tour). The up-tempo tune energized the sweltering crowd, and it presented Bono's second opportunity to leverage the Lennon sculpture as part of the performance—this time, by inserting some impromptu Beatles lyrics as a snippet. "In 'A Day Without Me,' we pull the root out of the song," Bono told UPI after the show. "And I just heard this melody, and it was, 'Dear Prudence, won't you come out to play, the sun is up, the sky is blue, it's beautiful and so are you,' and I felt that way about the crowd."[35] The U2Gigs.com database verifies that the US Festival was the first time U2 played "Dear Prudence" as a snippet, something the band would go on to do another six times over the next twenty-seven years.[36]

For this first time evoking the song, Bono's face was awash in a serene expression as he improvised a slight lyrical adjustment ("Well we've come here to play" replacing the original Lennon/McCartney lyric "Won't you come out to play"). Later in the day, Westwood One journalist Vicky McCarty (who would go on to marry future U2 collaborator Jimmy Iovine) asked Bono about the "Dear Prudence"

---

35 Metzler, Stan W. "'It Could Have Been Worse.'" UPI, May 31, 1983.

36 "Dear Prudence." U2Gigs.Com. December 8, 2010. https://www.u2gigs.com/Dear_Prudence-s152.html.

moment. In his answer, Bono doubled down on the claim that he did not previously know the Lennon sculpture would be on display.

Bono: "I just walked out on stage and there was this bronze statue of John Lennon."

McCarty: "That's amazing. So you weren't planning to do any sort of thing for John Lennon on the stage?"

Bono: "Oh God, no. I had no idea he was even on the stage."[37]

"An Cat Dubh" | The Sun's Still Shining

As the electricity of "A Day Without Me" cooled, Bono's remarks to the crowd included the aforementioned, "Nobody twisted my arm to come here. I'm here 'cause I *want* to be here." It has been suggested this was his subtle acknowledgment of the dark cloud the Clash had cast over the event on night one, when they made a giant step toward their eventual break-up on stage in front of an astonished US Festival audience.[38] It was the last time guitarist Mick Jones would play with the band he co-founded—and while Joe Strummer and Paul Simonon released a final record and toured as the Clash in 1985, the authoritative voice of *Rolling Stone* would later declare, "The Clash as we know them ended at the 1983 US Festival." [39] It remains a mystery whether Bono's "twisted my arm" remark was a public expression of disappointment with his punk heroes, but given the sequence of events the Clash had already set in motion, it's a safe bet.

Bono continued: "Firstly, can I say, we're an Irish band, alright? We plan on being here for a long time — forever, maybe. This is 'The Black Cat,' 'An Cat Dubh.'"

Only four songs in, Bono seized on this *Boy* track as a vehicle to show solidarity with his first-ever American summer festival

---

37 "Bono US Festival Interview 1983 U2." Historic Films Stock Footage Archive. September 23, 2013. Video, https://www.youtube.com/watch?v=ZAg-AZDTxqA

38 Boyd, Glen. "The Rockologist: Remembering The 1983 US Festival." BlogCritics.Org. March 14, 2009. https://doi.org/https://blogcritics.org/the-rockologist-remembering-the-1983-us/

39 Greene, Andy. "Flashback: The Clash Say Goodbye at the 1983 US Festival." *Rolling Stone*, November 1, 2012. https://www.rollingstone.com/music/music-news/flashback-the-clash-say-goodbye-at-the-1983-us-festival-57636/.

crowd—in Southern California, no less, the fabled land of endless summers. His audience connection efforts began after the second verse, with an attempt to mirror the thousands of young men in attendance by removing his own shirt and pulling a bright blue Puma ball cap onto his head. As the shaggy blonde stagehand he snatched the hat from looked on with bewilderment, the facial affect of the singer was what his fans now recognize as that of quintessential young Bono. Next, as the band prepared to transition to "Into the Heart," Bono ended "An Cat Dubh" with a unique, improvised coda that has never been duplicated since in any U2 performance:

"The sun's still shining … the sun's still shining on me today, this afternoon."

The song concluded with Bono gazing, seemingly in wonderment, at the sea of 200,000 faces. The audience was seeing in the making the definitive stage persona Bono was crafting for himself, one he would eventually refer to as "The Showman."

"Surrender" | The Ascension

The first *War* song of the set, "New Year's Day," was not introduced as such, although the track happened to be sitting at number sixty-two on the Billboard Hot 100 that week (the first U2 single to chart in the U.S.). It seems inconceivable that manager Paul McGuinness would not communicate this to the band—and yet, what would become one of U2's most recognizable classics for the next forty years was performed with minimal flourish on May 30, 1983. Instead, any pageantry was reserved for the next song, introduced by Bono this way: "There's a lot of real rubbish going on about new music and old music. Can I just say, we play U2 music. Is that OK? From an LP titled *War*, a song titled 'Surrender.'"

The title of this song remains a core U2 tenet to this day, as evidenced by the title of Bono's 2022 memoir (*Surrender: 40 Songs, One Story*); his fifteen-city speaking tour throughout 2022 and 2023 to promote the book (*Stories of Surrender*, which became a film streamed on Apple TV+ in 2025); and the band's controversial album of "re-imagined" U2 songs in 2023 (*Songs of Surrender*).

At the US Festival, "Surrender" marked the moment when Bono first chose to ascend to an impressive yet unreasonable height in order to connect with the audience. In so doing, he unwittingly put the entire security staff on warning—and although the optics were delightful, as anyone watching the footage online more than forty years later might observe, the antics were dangerous. A person who spoke on condition of anonymity who worked security that day recalled, "When Bono climbed the stage scaffolding, we were told by the security manager to let him hit the stage if he falls: 'Dumbass does that, don't get killed trying to break his fall.' If someone was to be a hero to catch him, the catcher would have been hurt worse than the faller." To make matters worse for the inconvenienced stagehands, they would soon realize that it was only Bono's first ascent of the performance. As for the crowd, they eagerly ate up his antics, which is exactly what Bono wanted. During the song, a camera panned to a homemade banner with the simple declaration, "Thank God for U2."

"Two Hearts Beat as One" | Angeline (the Bikini Girl)

U2 famously eluded the sexual enticements of the groupie phenomenon—but from early on, Bono heartily embraced the rock 'n roll trope of pulling a female from the audience onstage. The most oft-cited example is at Live Aid—where not just one, but *two* young women were selected to dance with Bono during "Bad," the second and final song of the band's truncated set on July 13, 1985. Two years before that, the aforementioned Red Rocks performance featured a parka-clad fan dancing with Bono in the Colorado cold. But the US Festival, held the week before Red Rocks, was far from the Denver rain. In the dustbowl of Devore, Bono welcomed onstage a California girl whose assertive energy epitomized the early 80s (as did her summer fashion: blonde curls, a bikini top, and low-rise jeans with a button-down shirt tied to the waist).

"I want *you*," he said as he pointed to her. At that, she was quickly hoisted over the barricade and onstage. With breasts bouncing and hair that sprung in sync with Bono's steps, she swept one arm up and down, her other arm pinned around his torso. When Bono launched into his snippet of Chubby Checkers' "Let's

Twist," they attempted to dance together while still entwined, which made for an awkward sight—and yet, he appeared to enjoy the entanglement as he continued to sing. She can't necessarily be faulted for not singing along; although the song had been released as a single in the U.S. two months prior in March, "Two Hearts" never charted on the Billboard 100. Furthermore, it is not known whether she was a U2 fan to begin with; she could have been there for Bowie, Stevie Nicks, Berlin, or any number of other performers.

In any case, Angeline—who identified herself after the song, once she was deposited back into the crowd—was called "beautiful" by Bono in his Westwood One interview after the show. "I want to marry her; no, I don't want to marry her," he said.[40] He and Ali had been married for nine months at that point; time and again over the decades, it has been documented that *War* was the album conceived during the couple's honeymoon.[41]

"Sunday Bloody Sunday" | Not a Rebel Song

"For this next song, there has been a lot of talk, probably too much talk. This is not a rebel song; this is 'Sunday Bloody Sunday.'" It would not be the first time Bono gave this familiar introduction to the song that U2's most devoted fans now simply refer to as "SBS," nor would it be the last.

The subject matter that formed the song's historical backdrop, which happened more than 5,000 miles away from California in 1972, was likely high over the heads of this crowd of teens and twenty-somethings in 1983. In fact, it would be another four years until a San Francisco crowd would witness Bono's ninety-second rant against a fan named Robert Quinn for holding up a homemade sign that said "SF+U2."[42]

Quinn, a psychedelic artist still residing in San Francisco, had intended for the sign to signal his city's affinity for U2—not, as Bono evidently thought at the time, to convey support for the Sinn Féin

---

40 Bono US Festival Interview 1983 U2." Historic Films Stock Footage Archive. September 23, 2013. Video, https://www.youtube.com/watch?v=ZAg-AZDTxqA.

41 McCormick, Neil. 2006. *U2 by U2*. Harper Collins.

42 O'Brien, Shane. "Fan Recounts when "Clueless" Bono Mistook His San Francisco Sign for Sinn Féin Support." Irish Central, June 7, 2023.

wing of the Irish Republican Army. If a sophisticated San Francisco audience was unaware that "SF" was also the abbreviation for the perpetrators of the 1987 Remembrance Day Bombing in Northern Ireland, then it seems unlikely that the origin story of "Sunday Bloody Sunday" would be fully understood by camped-out festival goers in San Bernardino (notoriously a less cosmopolitan region), just two months after the song's release in 1983.

Regardless, there was a sea of synchronized clapping as the crowd dutifully chanted the "No more!" antiphon that Bono had begun employing while performing the song on the *War* tour (a call and response that has become an expected component in live performances of "Sunday Bloody Sunday" over the decades). When viewing the footage online, Bono can be seen strutting across the stage holding the white flag of surrender prop; seconds later, the bikini-clad Angeline from the previous song—who may or may not have been a U2 fan before that day—can be seen waving both her fists.

"The Electric Co." | Climbing Jacob's Ladder

After remaining at the towel-draped mic stand for the first verse and kneeling at the tip of the stage for the second verse, Bono again grabbed the white flag. Up to this point of the *War* tour, the flag was often reserved for "Sunday Bloody Sunday" exclusively. Its use as a prop during other songs debuted at this moment of the US Festival, when it would simultaneously present another security challenge. The scenario commenced with Bono hoisting the flag onto his shoulder, prepared for yet another ascent up the scaffolding.

If there was a moment when all bets were off and the singer went on autopilot, this was it. Using the swinging rope ladder (also known as a "Jacob's ladder") meant for festival crew, he climbed to the highest point of the structure. When viewing the footage online, one observes Bono's facial expression growing more purposeful with every ladder rung.

One can speculate whether the scaffolding-climbing Bono of 1983 was inspired by the biblical story in the twenty-eighth chapter of Genesis, in which Jacob dreams of climbing a ladder to heaven. However, there was a potential reference to these US Festival antics forty years later during *U2:UV Achtung Baby Live at Sphere*.

Incorporated as a coda tacked onto the end of the song "Who's Gonna Ride Your Wild Horses," Bono repeated variations of a mantra that included the words "climbing up Jacob's ladder" on many nights throughout the residency. As he recited this coda, the screen graphic behind the band would morph into a massive, ladder-like structure of white light. Given U2's well-documented proclivity for cryptically incorporating earlier life experiences into U2's live stage elements, it seems entirely plausible this was an intentional "Easter egg" reference to the scaffolding he ascended four decades prior at the US Festival.

Jacob's Ladder in *U2:UV*, 2023
Photo by Brook W. Flagg

As the band continued to play "The Electric Co." bridge, Bono reached the top of the scaffolding, catapulted his corded mic over it during the song's instrumental bridge—and then, unbelievably, retrieved the mic in the nick of time before his vocals resumed. The crowd went nuts when he emerged, mic securely back in hand, over the top of the structure to sing a paraphrased version of the "Send in the Clowns" snippet often used in the song and yelling the declaration, "California, here I come!" This seemed an appropriate apex for such a performance—and yet, Bono was not finished. There was one more element to the stunt, and it involved maximizing the prop capability of the white flag.

It went like this: Bono trapezed from the rope ladder to the stationary ladder that led to the top of the scaffolding, carrying the flag toward the open sky. Then, at the risk of impaling the very audience members who cheered him on, he hurled it straight into the throng of excited new fans like an ancient warrior spear. It was reckless, rogue, rebellious—everything a twenty-three-year-old Bono aspired to be.

A May 31, 1983 UPI report recapped the stunt with Bono's own insights on his state of mind: *U-2 lead singer Paul 'Bono' Hewson electrified the crowd when he carried a white flag to the top of the six-story stage overhang and flung it into the crowd. 'I'm terrified of heights, actually, but I wanted to put that flag up to the top of the festival,' Hewson said. 'It's the principle of surrender, of giving of ourselves, not just between nations but between people on all levels.'*[43]

The flag landed, no one was hurt, and the crowd went wild. Bono, he was still at the top of the scaffolding as Edge, Adam, and Larry wound down the song; they attempted to give their singer the extra seconds needed to get out of the precarious position in which he had quite literally put himself. *How the hell was he going to get down from there?* Quickly and confidently, it turned out, with long-suffering tour manager Dennis Sheehan trailing his every move. As his face beamed with pride, Bono took a victorious bow. This incredible stunt—pulled off at a festival that has received only marginal attention in U2's career retrospectives over the decades—was Bono's most elaborate stage feat yet. Even so, the Red Rocks performance one week later would go on to earn substantially more acclaim. Perhaps it's simply a matter of exposure.

In his 2022 memoir, Bono made a brief reference to the US Festival and credited the spirit of John Lennon as his primary inspiration for the scaffolding stunt. "I wouldn't have been climbing to the top of the rigging on a festival stage holding the white flag if I hadn't been thinking of John's foolish acts of peace," he wrote.[44]

"I Will Follow" | The Crowd Goes Wild

Despite some periodic fluctuation, it is a generally accepted estimation that "I Will Follow" is the U2 song played live more times than any other. According to U2Gigs.com, "Pride (In the Name of Love)" overtook the distinction in 2017; however, site administrators acknowledge that "I Will Follow" has been played in a sufficient number of undocumented sets to remain the top-played song in U2 history. One administrator communicated (via the platform now

---

43 Metzler, Stan W. "'It Could Have Been Worse'." UPI, May 31, 1983.

44 Bono. 2022. *Surrender: 40 Songs, One Story.* Penguin Random House.

known as X) on June 20, 2017, "IWF likely 150 ahead still...To be more precise, I am 99% certain that 130 currently unknown sets had 'I Will Follow.' Repeat performances mean total plays may be >160."[45]

When the band played the '83 US Festival, the song had been a reliable radio hit for two years—and although it didn't crack the Billboard Hot 100, it reached number twenty on Billboard's Mainstream Rock chart in April 1981. It would soon enjoy a second wave of popularity upon the release of *Under a Blood Red Sky* in November, six months after the festival.

When watching the US Festival footage, it becomes clear that the crowd recognized what they were hearing. Cheering can be heard when the band returned to the stage for the encore and Edge's two-string opening riff commenced (as if Bono shouting, "Ladies and gentlemen, I will follow!" didn't tip them off more immediately). Viewers can also see that Adam and Larry contributed vocals (as was periodically the case in early tours), or at least appeared to, during the "walk away" repetition in the chorus of the song. "Hey mister," Bono repeatedly said to a festival worker during the "your eyes" bridge of the song. He was engaging in a bit of wordplay to prompt the worker, who was in fact misting the crowd with an industrial fire cannon hose, to do the same to him. Eventually, the worker saw where this was going and simply handed the hose over to Bono. Then—in what might be his most erotically suggestive stage antics at that point in his performance career—Bono held the hose up in the air so that the erupting stream delivered a dramatic, multi-sensory experience to the fans surrounding him. The crowd ate it up, cheering powerfully as the song ended and the band briefly separated from their instruments to give the illusion that the encore was over.

"40" | "Give Peace a Chance"

The encore was *not* over; "40," not "I Will Follow," had closed nearly every U2 show on the *War* tour thus far. As the band's US Festival performance neared its end, there was one final interaction between

---

45   Matkin, @U2Gigs, "IWF likely 150 ahead still...To be more precise, I am 99% certain that 130 currently unknown sets had 'I Will Follow.' Repeat performances mean total plays may be >160." Twitter (now X, June 20, 2017. (Deleted).

Bono and the Lennon statue: "Hey John, how about one more?" Prompted by the cheering crowd, Bono then gave what is arguably the most beloved closing song in U2 history its familiar introduction, albeit with an uncharacteristic stammer: "This … this is … this is '40'."

Throughout most of the tour, the "40" introduction began with "Good night"—but U2's US Festival performance was in the afternoon. The crowd wasn't going anywhere; the Pretenders, Stevie Nicks, and David Bowie would all play before the night was over.

As he walked off for the progressive exit that has traditionally accompanied "40" as a closer throughout U2's career, Bono appeared to have an epiphany. When viewing the footage, this can be seen on a backstage camera that captured the moment. Before the band members exited, Bono spun on his heels, returned to the stage, and cradled the mic to sing the chorus of Lennon's 1969 anthem "Give Peace a Chance" in a higher key than the original recording. The crowd intuitively joined in. Later in the Westwood One interview, Bono appeared emotional recalling the moment: "When I started to walk back and the crowd started to chant 'Give Peace a Chance'...I mean, what can you say?"[46]

Finally, as it often has throughout U2 history, "40" ended with the sound of audience members chanting the "How long to sing this song" refrain. The transition was likely initiated over the speakers, a brilliant production element dreamed up by tour manager Dennis Sheehan. And with that, U2's first American festival performance concluded.

Shaping the Course of a Career

Perhaps it's unfair to place the US Festival side-by-side with Red Rocks and demand that fans choose which is U2's "true" American breakthrough. Both powerfully shaped the course of the band's career at a time when their profile in the States was being elevated by increased radio airplay and the rise of MTV. There were stark differences between the two shows—including, but not limited to, the most basic conditions of geography and weather. Red Rocks was an early June evening drenched in rain—while on the afternoon of

---

46 "Bono US Festival Interview 1983 U2." Historic Films Stock Footage Archive. September 23, 2023. Video,

May 30, the sun shone on U2 in a uniquely glorious fashion that has not been duplicated since in more than forty years. It was a moment in time that will never happen again, and it could only happen in Southern California.

"I won't forget today," Bono told Westwood One. "And I hope other people won't either."[47]

US Festival | U2 Fan Memories

There were 670,000 people in attendance for the weekend, and estimates for day three have topped 200,000. A few U2 fans who were in attendance, including those who came from long distances as young people to attend the festival, shared their memories for this book.

Dave Burton | Vancouver, Canada

It was 1983, and U2 was huge that year in Canada. I was a teen working at some phone sales job, and would stop in to Sam the Record Man to buy my weekly albums. They had a draw to win tickets to a three-day concert in California, and I took a whole book of fifty tickets and shoved them in my pocket to fill out later. I came back the next weekday, crammed them all in the little draw box, and got a live call a few weeks later from CFOX, the local rock station, saying I had won. I wasn't actually old enough to win, so I had filled out my older brother's name and he 'invited' me as his guest. At the time, it was about a $5,000 package.

It was our first time in California, and we were so excited. We brought a tent and pitched it on the grass somewhere. U2 was fantastic; I remember Bono climbed way up on top, over the stage—and later, dancing with a lady from the audience. It was incredibly hot that day, and they had fire cannon hoses spraying us all. I'll never forget being in that atmosphere of 300,000 fans. I brought back a t-shirt with all the bands on it and wore it out at my high school because I was so proud of having gone. I often rewatch the U2 clips on YouTube, and it brings back such powerful emotions of being young and feeling so free. U2, and their early music especially, will always be such a huge part of that for me.

---

47 Ibid.

Ken Wong | Los Angeles, CA > Tucson, AZ

I was already a huge U2 fan before the festival. I was working at Tower Records in West Covina and we had Ticketron there, so I had the inside scoop on how to get tickets. The key was convincing my mom to let me go for four days and stay over. Once I figured that out, we filled my friend's Pinto with sleeping bags, camping gear, and jugs of Sparkletts (plus whatever we could get at the 7-Eleven).

It was desert hot and super dusty on Edge's side of the stage, but I was near a water cannon, and the sound was much better on the left side. The people around me had no idea who the statue on the stage was supposed to be until I mentioned that it was John Lennon. I remember Bono climbing up, and at the time, it seemed so long for him to get up there. I'm not sure he realized how tall the scaffolding was, and the crew was freaking out on the ground as they realized the mic cord wasn't long enough. Because of the angle we had, I could see there was no platform to rest that flag on—so, 100% it was going to fall over the back. It felt like an eternity.

During "Two Hearts," there was this super hyper girl that Bono brought up. She kind of ruined that song for me, as she was super bouncy and very distracting. The set was slightly shorter than most of the bands from day one—and I kinda wished they were on day one, as I think it wouldn't have been a better fit—but overall, it was a good show.

Jan Sandys-Renton | San Diego, CA > El Segundo, CA

I went with my friend Becky. It wasn't our first concert, but certainly our first festival. Both of us were into the San Diego punk scene and went to a lot of small venues to see bands like the Dead Kennedys, 45 Grave, and The Cramps—but we were both very excited to see one of the fathers and influencers, David Bowie. We only had tickets for Monday; I remember having to park quite far away, and we walked along an elevated railroad track to get to the festival entrance. Along the way, we were offered every drug under the sun and got quite a few cat calls. Neither of us were old enough to drink, and we were not there to alter our minds in any way (we wouldn't risk misremembering any moment of Bowie's performance). It was a hot day; I remember minimal clothing on people and bottles of water being expensive.

Because a friend had played the Boy and War albums for me and we had seen U2 videos on MTV, we were familiar with U2's music and excited to see them live. "I Will Follow" has been one of my favorite songs since seeing them perform it that day, but their entire performance was electric! Between Bono climbing the scaffolding, him dancing with a girl from the crowd, and the band's non-stop energy, it was easy to see that they were going to be something big. I recall getting goosebumps from the energy that day. With no cell phones at that time and no cameras allowed, all we have now are our memories.

Jeanette Narciso | Wildomar, CA

I was few months pregnant with my second son, who is now thirty-nine! When we arrived and got a view of all the people who were already there, our reaction was "Wow"—but we were more in awe at how huge this stage setup was. For those times, it was massive, in both height and length. We found a spot on a hill close to the speaker stacks, so about 150 feet from the stage. I remember the event promoter talked to the crowd and introduced Steve Wozniak; he talked about Apple, which was just entering the computer tech fold. Wozniak spoke so joyfully about the promising future we all had ahead and the technical revolution to come. There was a life-size bronze statue of John Lennon off to the right side of the stage. Woz said the festival was dedicated to the memory of him, and how going forward, we need to live as John lived: "All you need is love." Next, he introduced "the new rock sensation" ... U2!

When they opened with "Gloria," we both looked at each other with big smiles. Imagine hearing, "This is Gloria. Two, three, four!" You hear Edge's howling guitar riffs while Larry and Adam are pounding the beat. Then Bono does what he does, commanding the audience to sing. It was perfection. As both of us were Catholic-raised and married, we truly thought we were hearing a voice of God. I don't know how to explain the energy that took over the entire festival when they started playing. To say it was "elevated" was not enough; I'm talking about a collective energy that I have only ever felt at a U2 concert. It's like a burst at your atomic core. We all felt it.

Los Angeles Sports Arena

Location: 3939 South Figueroa Street, Los Angeles

Significance: First arena show headlined by U2 anywhere in the world; site of Bono's infamous balcony jump, a turning point for both him and the band

Date in U2 history: June 17, 1983

Still in operation/visitable? No

Building still standing? No

"This was a tipping point for Bono. It would never be the same again."
— Bill See, *Into the Heart of U2 Podcast*, 2023[48]

The night of June 17, 1983 bears the distinction of being the first time U2 would headline an arena anywhere in the world. It was their second visit to the venue; the first time (March 27, 1982, on the fourth leg of the *October* tour), they were the opening act for the J. Geils Band. But now, U2 was the main event. They were supported by The Alarm, who joined the tour in Salt Lake City on June 3.

The set began with "Out of Control," as it had on the previous five North American stops. When the song concluded, Bono acknowledged the stark contrast between the US Festival a few weeks earlier and the comparative grandeur of playing their largest indoor venue to date. "A few weeks ago, we played in a large field about fifty miles from here," he told the crowd—using the slow, distinctly enunciated cadence that has come to be associated with the young Bono's speaking style. "Now, now we're playing a large sports complex."

Setting the tone for the night—and for that matter, the next forty years—Bono stated his intent to create an atmosphere of intimacy in the arena. "It's our mission tonight to turn this large

48 See, Bill. "War (Part 2)." https://Podcasts.Apple.Com/Us/Podcast/War-part-2/
    Id1706044037?I=1000630442014. Apple Podcasts, October 6, 2023.

building into a small room," he said. "And I think that maybe we've already done that. Thank you."[49]

A Line is Drawn

Headlining an arena for the first time was a major achievement, but this June evening in 1983 holds significance in U2's live performance history for a second (and arguably more critical) reason. Held only three weeks after Bono impulsively scaled to the top of the massive Jacob's ladder at the US Festival in San Bernardino, the *War* tour's LA Sports Arena show was the night during which U2's biggest stakeholders drew a hard, uncompromising line. It was a boundary necessary to the very survival of the band: the life of its singer.

On an episode of *Into the Heart of U2 Podcast* recapping this pivotal stretch of the *War* tour, co-host Bill See explained, "Tour manager Dennis Sheehan and the band were becoming increasingly concerned [Bono] was going to get himself killed or paralyzed."

Co-host Melody Muraca agreed. "I mean, the band at this point, they put their foot down that he needs to stop."

"They begged him," See said. "But he wasn't listening, or he couldn't hear, once he got onstage…This was a tipping point for Bono. It would never be the same again."[50]

Indeed, things would never be the same after the events of that evening. Here is a patchworked retelling of the storied summer night when stagecraft antics that could only happen in LA present-ed an undeniable crossroads for U2.

Feeling the Weight

For those who have followed U2's nearly five decades of performing for live audiences of all sizes, it's a reasonable conclusion: With each new level of success the band attains, Bono feels pressured to do *more*: more theatrics, more vocal crescendos, more audience connection. The June 17, 1983 show at the LA Sports Arena remains

---

49 "1983 06 17 Los Angeles, California Sports Arena." Adrian Newman. June 17, 2018.
     Video, https://www.youtube.com/watch?v=qAqkhltuTzw&list=RDqAqkhltuTzw&start_radio=1.

50 See, Bill. Muraca, Melody. "War (Part 2)."
     https://Podcasts.Apple.Com/Us/Podcast/War-part-2/Id1706044037?I=1000630442014.
     Apple Podcasts, October 6, 2023.

a paragon signifying how acutely that pressure can manifest in his performance.

To make an analogy to a performance from a more recent era, it could be said that this show is to the *War* tour what the November 2, 2023 show was to the *U2:UV Achtung Baby Live at Sphere* residency. In the latter example, it was the night Bono began immersing himself into the crowd during "Until the End of the World," the sixth song in the predictable first half of the set, as he had during *ZooTV*. He would wait two months into the *U2:UV* shows to incorporate the maneuver, perhaps until the security climate of the high-profile Las Vegas residency had become more predictable. But once he went for it, it was a gusto-filled routine that, many nights, included the over-the-top gimmick of playfully biting a gleefully consenting fan on the hand.

Although there were no vampiric antics forty years earlier at the LA Sports Arena, Bono still embedded himself into the crowd so deeply that night in 1983 that it generated utter terror among his bandmates and management. See and Muraca, both in attendance that night as young fans, described their recollections of how it began. "It really became clear from the onset that Bono felt the weight of this being their first headlining arena show," See explained. "It was obvious, like, from the get-go; he had his mind set on getting to the people at the back of the arena. It felt palpable."

The Biggest "Something"

"The moment that was probably the most memorable was during 'Electric Co.,'" Muraca recalled. "And maybe because he was playing the biggest show they'd ever done, he was going to do the biggest 'something' that he'd ever done during that song." Although there are no known videos of the show in circulation, an audio recording on YouTube confirms significant audience participation during "The Electric Co.," particularly after the second verse.[51]

It would not be unusual for "something" to happen during this part of the song, as it was a point in the show that Bono had actively played with night after night. See reminded listeners of this fact: "All through the *War* tour, you know, he had been going

---

51 "1983 06 17 Los Angeles, California Sports Arena." Adrian Newman. June 17, 2018.
    Video, https://www.youtube.com/watch?v=qAqkhltuTzw&list=RDqAqkhltuTzw&start_radio=1.

into the audience during 'Electric Co.'—climbing balconies, scaling, scaffolding, anything to reach the audience that felt further and further away as the venues got bigger." To all concerned (his three bandmates, plus manager Paul McGuiness and tour manager Dennis Sheehan), it likely seemed there was no way for Bono to top what he had pulled off while performing the song at the US Festival a few weeks prior. But they would be wrong.

When reviewing the audio recording, we can hear the band play the extended bridge after the second verse for more than two minutes before Bono resumes vocals. That alone would not necessarily set this performance of "The Electric Co." apart from any other night on the *War* tour's ambitious North American leg. What *does* set it apart starts just before Bono returns the mic to his lips to sing the familiar "two, three, four" refrain that introduced that night's variation on the "Send in the Clowns" snippet. At that point, there was a noticeable shift as the crowd can be heard cheering as though something truly remarkable was happening around them. But *what* was happening?

Everybody Wants to Be There

During their podcast discussion, Muraca and See hashed out how they each recall the night's events unfolding. Noting that the only media coverage was a single *Los Angeles Times* article and photo, there was, as See stated, "Not a great amount of consensus as to what happened. We're laughing, [because] it's almost biblical, like an oral tradition … for such an immortal show, that's actually a shocking lack of coverage."

Muraca recalled, "During 'The Electric Co.,' Bono's on the stage, he climbs up onto the PA and gets onto the first balcony, or the loge, with the white flag. And he starts making his way towards the center of the arena to get closer to the audience."

"From my vantage point," See interjected, "It felt like I didn't even know how he got off the stage and into the loge…But then he made his way to what's been called a balcony … to me, I think it was the aisle way in between the loge and the colonnade. And he had the white flag, and it seemed like this gesture where he was going to march with the white flag down this aisleway and lead people on this journey to the back of the arena. But of course, he never got there. And it was madness."

"He comes to a stop about mid-point in the arena," Muraca continued, "simply because he has to. And I think not everybody knew where he was until that point ... everyone wants to get close to him. He's getting what he wants, and everybody wants to be there. And he gets stuck, literally, by the crush of the crowd. There's nowhere else for him to go."

She recalls that the white flag was ripped away from Bono by a crowd member, followed by a lot of pushing, shoving, and pulling on shirts. "All of a sudden, people are stealing this flag because they want a piece of it, and they want a piece of *him*. And it was ... not great."

See continued, "He tries to escape this crush by going down an aisle that leads to the railing, which is the loge, and then the next step is the floor. And I guess at that point, he had nowhere else to go. People were following him down this aisle like this trail of ants, just converging on him ... And ultimately, he looks down, and the hands are raised up to catch him, and he literally jumps."

And just like that—in one impulsive move made necessary by a sheer lack of options—everyone in U2's orbit who thought Bono couldn't top his US Festival stunt was proven wrong. He had just leapt off a fifteen-foot balcony, trusting that the outstretched arms of the fans below would catch him (which, basically, they did).

As for Edge, Adam, and Larry, they simply continued to play the song. They were used to this by now, whether they liked it or not. "That was a long ass time of the band just going on the coda of 'Electric Co.,'" See observed. "They must have been thinking, 'Oh, Bono's just fucked off. What do we do now?' No wonder Dennis Sheehan and the band confronted him afterwards."

"One of the Most Dramatic Things I've Ever Seen"

Once again, *Los Angeles Times* music reporter Robert Hilburn was in attendance to review U2's stop in the city. This time, he bluntly summarized their performance as "frequently breathtaking, but not always in the most positive sense."[52]

---

52 Hilburn, Robert. "U2 in Concert." Los Angeles Times, June 20, 1983.

"U2 lead singer Paul 'Bono' Hewson shared his aims and frustrations with the Sports Arena crowd with the broad, open gestures of a charismatic missionary," Hilburn wrote. "Hewson wants badly to stir his audience on the same deeply emotional level that bands like the Beatles and Who once touched him, that he sometimes succumbed to clumsy, exaggerated devices."

It seems Hilburn also wondered just where the singer had gone during the instrumental portion of "The Electric Co." In describing the perplexing scenario that played out, Hilburn wrote, "Hewson reappeared, with the white flag and staff, on the arena's second [balcony] level. The idea was idealistic enough. He wanted to create a symbolic bond with the audience by having fans march along with him. But Hewson only got six feet before a guy, obviously more concerned with souvenirs than symbolism, yanked the flag from the staff and raced away. So much for idealism."

As for jumping off the second-story balcony into the welcoming arms of the crowd? "One of the most dramatic things I've ever seen a pop star do," Hilburn wrote. "It was also one of the most questionable." Hilburn pointed out that at least two fans ("other young men," he wrote) followed Bono off the balcony, and no one below was concerned about catching *them*. "The fans didn't appear to be hurt," he wrote, "and thank goodness, everyone else had the good sense not to follow their lead."[53]

Ultimately, the amalgamation of Hilburn's review with multiple warnings from his bandmates and management prompted Bono to stop viewing his body as an inconvenience meant to be overcome with careless actions.

In *U2 at the End of the World*, Bill Flanagan wrote of the incident: "The band organized a series of courts martial at which they chewed him out for endangering himself and any kids in the crowd who might try to imitate him. He finally got the message when Edge, Adam, and Larry threatened to break up U2 if he didn't stop making like Tarzan. Bono told me at the time that he was also influenced by a concert review written by Robert Hilburn in the *LA Times* in which the critic said that U2's music didn't need such

_____

53 Hilburn, Robert. "U2 - A Breathtaking Force for the Future." *Los Angeles Times*, June 20, 1983.

distractions. I think Hilburn has remained Bono's conservative conscience over the years."[54]

As for Bono's own account of the event, it shows some personal resistance to the idea that his extreme performance antics stopped with this show—or, that they ever stopped at all. In chapter 26 of *Surrender*—the portion of his memoir devoted to the ostentation of his onstage theatrics titled "The Showman," after the *Songs of Experience* track of the same name—Bono wrote:

"At the Los Angeles Sports Arena in 1983, I climbed up onto a balcony with a white flag to make some point about pacifism, and when someone tried to pull the flag out of my hand ... I started beating him off with my fists ... Then I jumped off the balcony in what one critic called one of the most stupid stunts he'd ever seen.

You could call it showboating. It is, but I also call it the search for a physical symbolism...Breaking down the barrier between performer and fan ... Edge, or Larry, or Adam or someone in management will periodically intervene, extracting a promise that I will not get carried away like this...

But that's the point. Music carries us away ... It's a symbol of what is really taking place, which is that this audience are still carrying this band after forty years."

– Bono, *Surrender: 40 Songs, One Story*, 2022[55]

The Lasting Legacy of the Arena

Just as the Los Angeles Sports Arena holds a special place in U2 history, U2 held a special place in the history of the venue because of this night. Although it was nearly twenty-five years old by 1983, the Sports Arena—which was in operation from 1959 through its demolition in 2016—had never before allowed festival seating for a rock show until the night that U2 headlined (according to Hilburn's knowledge at the time). Today, chairs on the general admission floor seem utterly preposterous at a U2 show, whether indoors or out. To

54 Flanagan, Bill. 1996. *U2 at the End of the World*. Penguin Random House.

55 Bono. 2022. *Surrender: 40 Songs, One Story*. Penguin Random House.

that end, the Los Angeles Sports Arena set in motion what would remain the standard audience setup at every U2 performance for the rest of their career.

The Most Extraordinary Moment

To conclude their reflections, the *Into the Heart of U2 Podcast* hosts each shared poignant summations of the night that came to define the collective experience of so many Southern California-based U2 fans during the early 80s (9,633 fans, according to show attendance figures posted to U2tours.com).[56]

"I think that was probably the most exciting thing I've ever seen," Muraca said with a note of wistfulness. She added that it would be wrong for critics to be dismissive of the balcony stunt that led to the abrupt, yet necessary ending of this phase in Bono's evolution as a performer. "I don't think somebody who is literally balancing on a balcony railing, which is what he was doing in boots, was just theatrics," she said. "And there were no nets."

Indeed, Bono was "possessed by a kind of otherness" that night, See stated. "That was the end of *that* version of Bono the performer," he said, "which, frankly, a part of me does miss."

I've seen hundreds of shows since," he added. "And to this day, it's the most extraordinary moment I've ever witnessed."[57]

---

56 "U2 Concert: Jun 17, 1983 at Los Angeles , CA." U2tours.Com.

57 See, Bill. Muraca, Melody. "War (Part 2)."

U2 IN CONCERT

Continued from First Page

that he sometimes succumbed to clumsy, exaggerated devices. At one point, he carried a white flag of peace on a staff to the front of the stage with a determination reminiscent of the men who planted the flag on Iwo Jima.

Leaving the stage later during an instrumental break, Hewson reappeared, with the white flag and staff, on the arena's second (balcony) level. The idea was idealistic enough. He wanted to create a symbolic bond with the audience by having fans march along with him.

But Hewson only got six feet before a guy, obviously more concerned with souvenirs than with symbolism, yanked the flag from the staff and raced away. So much for idealism.

Eager to find another way to break down the barrier between performer and audience, Hewson climbed over the balcony and dropped about 10 to 15 feet into the arms of fans on the ground level. One of the most dramatic things I've ever seen a pop star do, it was also one of the most questionable.

At least two other young men followed Hewson's lead and, monkey-see style, also leaped from the balcony. Only this time there were no outstretched arms to greet them. The fans didn't appear to be hurt and, thank

goodness, everyone else had the good sense not to follow their lead.

The final breathtaking element of the concert dealt with the hundreds of fans pressed so tightly against the front of the stage that dozens finally climbed onto the stage for safety. Others simply climbed on stage to show off—an increasingly common practice at new-wave gatherings.

This was, I believe, the first time the Sports Arena has allowed festival seating (no chairs on the main floor) for a rock show. And, some in the audience maintain that the constant parade of fans across the stage adds a sense of adventure to the proceedings.

When you have music as exciting and as purposeful as U2's, however, you really don't need a sideshow as well, especially a potentially dangerous one. Make no mistake: This group is shaping up as one of *the* great bands of the '80s.

Robert Hilburn

6/17/83

Los Angeles Times

SECTION II

The
Sacred
Sites
of   *The Joshua Tree*

An Innocent Messenger
Essay by the author

In 2020—a year widely recognized as a time period teetering on the threshold of hell—I experienced a few distressing life events, the converging of which triggered something resembling an existential crisis. Maybe you did too.

Over the next few years, I sought comfort and insight from an eclectic pool of resources. Floating in that metaphorical self-help hot tub was a growing stack of half-finished books by popular Instagram therapists; my heavy rotation of in-person sessions with helpful licensed clinicians; and in addition to semi-annual excursions to U2 sites throughout Southern California with friends regarded as "U2 sisters" (the inspiration for this book), there were a handful of impulsive solo turnaround trips, most of which were wasted on uncontrolled sobbing. Finally, rounding out my self-prescribed protocol was a scheduled chat with an intuitive psychic medium.

This was not my first rodeo with a medium. It was, however, my first reading with a medium who was not a straight white woman in her 50s through 70s with wild hair and a chunky statement necklace.

This time, my medium was a clean-shaven gay man who didn't look a day over thirty-five. He came highly recommended, I was drawn to where he resided, and his media portfolio was impressive. It was enough to feel cautiously optimistic about investing an hour of my life and a reasonable, going-rate fee in exchange for his time and talents.

Plus, his bio was wild. It offered an abundance of fascinating credentials, such as:
- "Hereditary precognitive clairvoyant, sixth in line in a family of clairaudient clairsentients"
- "At age sixteen, hired by a city police department in LA County to help solve local homicides"
- "Performed earth healing at the DMZ North Korean border while serving in the Army"

The intrigue was irresistible. So I bit.

Our conversation was in August 2023. A small part of it is relevant to this chapter, starting with this prognostication.

"You're working on a book," he said.

Wow. This guy's good. "I am," I replied.

"It's something about music. Like, a band?"

We were more than halfway through our session at that point, and he had already demonstrated impressive, unnatural knowledge about other personal details I hadn't come prepared to talk about. His intuition was spot-on—so after the other revelations he had uncovered, why not lean into this one? I subtly masked my astonishment with a mild, "It is."

His next reveal came with an adorable honesty. "I have to admit, I don't know many bands. But I like My Chemical Romance."

That confession made sense for an empathic millennial. I smiled. "Aw."

He kept going. "But I think it's someone a little older."

"It is." Wow. Stay calm.

He continued. "And it's almost like your book is … " He clenched his eyes shut while I waited, as if scanning the precognizant database in his brain for a specific word.

"It's not exactly like, but parts of it are going to be like … a scrapbook?"

Holy crap. I can't stay calm now. "Yes. Yes. Oh my God, YES."

I could have easily dismissed this as a hunch—or, scoured my online presence for whatever public details led him to form this conclusion (for what it's worth, there weren't enough out there for this level of detail). But if you're going to book a slot on a renowned psychic's waitlist more than a year in advance, it would be a waste of time to brush off his sapience with skepticism. Between his premonitions on this book and some other key insights about me, I was sold on his gifts. In that moment, he was my messenger.

Unfortunately, even the most angelic beings aren't omnipotent. For one, he didn't know this "older" band was U2 (after all, he was a millennial angel. That's a joke). But once I told him it was, he shared that he knew only a single key detail about the band.

"U2 … They have a thing about a Joshua tree, right?"

If it came from anyone else, a question like that could easily trigger my gatekeeping impulses. But he posed it with such innocent sincerity that those impulses melted away.

"They do," I answered. "They do have a thing about a Joshua tree." Yes, a record that won two Grammys is a "thing." I'd never had so much grace for a person inquiring about this band before, but to my surprise, I didn't even have to try. I loved the kind ingenuousness of his questions.

"I've heard that those trees only grow in, like, two places on earth? California and the Holy Land?"

"I've heard that too," I said.

That wasn't a lie. I *had* heard the idea that Joshua trees only grew in California and Israel. I may have even believed it at one time (and I would be in good company; as you'll soon learn, Bono himself believed it at one time).

"I'm not sure if it's true," I continued. And at the time, I wasn't.

The rest of the conversation isn't relevant here. Suffice it to say that from a series of innocent inquiries about U2, I learned the value of asking questions with a spirit of kind curiosity—and the value of answering questions with an equally gracious good faith, no matter the answer (for what it's worth, I was already in the beginning stages of learning both those things through some of the other resources I was seeking out at the time. But this

The Joshua Tree 2017 stage,
Rose Bowl
Photo by Brook W. Flagg

interaction felt less confrontational than the others). That was the message he conveyed—and whether it came directly from him or some other spirit guide, I try to carry it with me.

That brief experience in my life is relevant to this next section of the book. I know what you're thinking: *How, exactly?*

I know. It's been a few paragraphs.

It's the fable behind this messenger's question about where Joshua trees grow. Wherever he got the idea that they only grow in California and the Holy Land, suffice it to say that *many* people have believed that at some point, including the very person who wrote and sang every lyric on the 1987 record with this tree as its name. It's one of a few myths and mysteries we'll dissect as we explore the first sacred U2 sites in this book: The Sacred Sites of *The Joshua Tree*. Let's go there now.

The Sacred Sites of *The Joshua Tree*

Zabriskie Point

Location: Requires mobile navigation app in Death Valley National Park

Sacredness: Front album cover of *The Joshua Tree*

Date in U2 history: (Likely) December 15, 1986

Visitable? Yes

The Joshua Tree

Location: Off Highway 190, requires GPS coordinates + mobile navigation app

Sacredness: Back album cover of *The Joshua Tree*

Date in U2 history: (Likely) December 15, 1986

Visitable? Yes

"We then drove off, and I don't know if we'll ever find that Joshua tree again."

– Bono, *Propaganda no. 5*, 1987[58]

To dig into the mystique of the Joshua tree—from the plant species itself, to the one discovered by the four members of U2 and their travel caravan in December 1986, to the other notable Mojave Desert locations that make up the iconic album art of the record that bears the tree's name—is a deep excavation.

Today, U2's tree is rapidly disintegrating as it lies high on the desert plain from which it grew, sporadically surrounded by hundreds of younger trees from the highway to the hills. But on the art that accompanies every physical media copy of *The Joshua Tree* in circulation today, the tree remains forever frozen in monochrome

---

58 "The Joshua Tree." *Propaganda* No. 5, May 1, 1987.

as a promising lone growth that sprang up in the barren desert—healthy, robustly upright, and surrounded only by four Irish pilgrims.

The Ultimate U2 Road Trip

For those who follow U2 with devotional fervor, traveling to the Joshua tree immortalized on the back album cover is an experience like no other. When combined with a visit to the front album cover location at Zabriskie Point (the other sacred site of *The Joshua Tree*) and the multiple sites of significance in the next chapter, it makes for the ultimate U2 road trip. Over the next several pages, we will examine all these sites, along with the information needed to plan a proper pilgrimage.

The Joshua Tree: Myth & Mystery

U2's fifth studio album, *The Joshua Tree*, was released on March 9, 1987. Very quickly, it catapulted the band into global superstardom, delivered the members their first two Grammys (and four nominations), and triggered a wave of critical and cultural accolades, including the *Time* magazine appositive "Rock's Hottest Ticket," famously declared on the cover of the April 27, 1987 issue, shot by Neal Preston.[59]

Despite playing the part of "World's Biggest Band," that designation was not formally incorporated into media coverage of U2 until a few years later.[60] Murmurs of the title began with *Achtung Baby* and the *ZooTV* tour, then recessed a bit during the *Pop* album and *Popmart* tour era, only to return spectacularly when the turn-of-the-millennium timing of *All That You Can't Leave Behind* thrust them back onto the global radar. It was further propelled by the *Elevation* tour and their post-9/11 exposure in the two years that followed. But no matter when the title befell them, there is ample consensus—both critical and popular—that the

---

59 Cocks, Jay, and Elizabeth L. Bland. "U2: Band on the Run." "U2: Rock's Hottest Ticket," *Time Magazine*, April 27, 1987.

60 Saavedra, David. "U2: The Boom and Bust of the World's Biggest Band." *El Pais*, October 11, 2021. https://english.elpais.com/usa/2021-10-11/u2-the-boom-and-bust-of-the-worlds-biggest-band.html.

groundwork for U2's long-term success was firmly laid with *The Joshua Tree.*

The legacy of the record has maintained its strength through the decades. In 2014, the U.S. Library of Congress selected *The Joshua Tree* as one of twenty-five recordings designated for long-term preservation in the library's National Recording Registry because of cultural, historical, or aesthetic importance.[61] In 2017—thirty years after its release—it would be the first U2 album to be celebrated with its own anniversary tour. *The Joshua Tree 2017* generated $390 million in sales from its first four legs (the Americas and Europe) through a final leg (Oceania and Asia) in 2019. (Side note: an entirely different effort, the *Experience + Innocence* tour, bridged the gap in 2018 and generated $126.2 million in sales.) Even in the cynical streaming era, with unlimited platforms for retrospective music critics eager to pick apart the past, many who publicly chime in on U2 (supportively or otherwise) broadly acknowledge that *The Joshua Tree* made a permanent, undeniable impact on popular music.[62]

For casual U2 fans, *The Joshua Tree* tends toward a special place in memory; for serious U2 fans, it's held up as a holy grail. Yet somehow, aspects of its origin story—including details related to the tree it was named for—remain shrouded in just enough mystery to precipitate a few misunderstandings, even among devoted U2 followers who look to the record as a source of spiritual inspiration.

To clear up those misunderstandings and provide a cohesive overview of facts, what follows are some of the most common myths about the tree itself, and mysteries surrounding the folkloric trip on which it was discovered by U2, photographer Anton Corbijn, and the small crew that accompanied them across the California desert for a three-day road trip believed to take place over December 14–16, 1986.[63] *Note: The record will be referenced in title case as* The Joshua Tree, *while "the Joshua tree" will refer to the tree species.*

61 "U2's The Joshua Tree Tapped for Library of Congress Preservation." Associated Press. April 22, 2014.

62 Quinn, Rick. "Outside Is America: 35 Years After U2'S 'The Joshua Tree.'" Pop Matters. March 9, 2022.

63 "This Day in U2 History - December 14." U2songs.com. https://www.u2songs.com/history/12_14.

Mystery: Joshua Tree vs. Succulent Plant

In recent decades, full-band TV appearances have been relatively rare occurrences for U2. When they do happen, it's typically on late-night talk shows. During one such appearance (*Jimmy Kimmel Live*, May 23, 2017), Bono called the Joshua tree "our very own yucca plant."[64] He was correct; the Joshua tree is part of the yucca genus, species name *yucca brevifolia*. The National Park Service (NPS) documents one key indicator that the Joshua is more plant than tree: the absence of annual rings inside. "These 'trees' do not have growth rings like you would find in an oak or pine," states the NPS official website entry for Joshua trees. The page also points out that yucca brevifolia is a member of the agave family—and that until recently, it was considered "a giant member of the lily family."[65]

The Center for Biological Diversity adds another layer of complexity: "In the yucca genus, they're a type of grass-like flowering plant called a monocot."[66]

And the National Wildlife Federation deepens the mystery further before digging it up: "Joshua trees aren't actually trees— they're succulents, a type of plant that stores water. In their dry ecosystems, however, they are considered trees of the desert."[67] Although colloquially known as a tree, the flora identity of the Joshua tree requires a more uniform expert consensus—and until that consensus materializes, the classification remains a mystery.

Myth: California and the Holy Land

As underscored by the anecdote that precedes this chapter, one of the most pervasive myths surrounding the Joshua tree concerns its nativity. In the 2016 *Huffington Post* essay "Joshua Tree: Evading The Jaws Of Los Angeles Greed," writer Vita Lusty dispelled the widespread misconception that the spiritual significance of the

---

64 "Jimmy's Full Interview with U2." Jimmy Kimmel Live - Facebook. May 28, 2017. Video, https://www.facebook.com/watch/?v=10155312148708374.

65 Joshua Trees." NPS.gov. U.S. National Park Service, https://www.nps.gov/jotr/learn/nature/jtrees.htm#.

66 "Saving the Joshua Tree." BiologicalDiversity.Org. Center for Biological Diversity, https://www.nps.gov/jotr/learn/nature/jtrees.htm#.

67 Joshua Tree." NWF.org. National Wildlife Federation, https://www.nwf.org/Educational-Resources/Wildlife-Guide/Plants-and-Fungi/Joshua-Tree.

Joshua tree is a geographical connection to the Holy Land of the Bible by writing, "Many say it only grows at two ends of the Earth, in the Mojave Desert and in Israel. This is untrue. The Joshua tree only grows in the high Mojave Desert and low Colorado Desert."[68]

The NPS has clarified that while Joshua trees grow primarily in the Mojave, they can be found elsewhere throughout the western United States. On the agency's web page devoted to educating the public on the species, it states, "The Joshua tree provides a good indicator that you are in the Mojave Desert, but you may also find it growing next to a saguaro cactus in the Sonoran Desert in western Arizona, or mixed with pines in the San Bernardino Mountains." Other sources, including the U.S. Forest Service, further point to additional Joshua tree reserves outside California—and, even outside the U.S. The department's yucca brevifolia entry states, "Its distribution follows the Mojave Desert boundary in southern Nevada, southwestern Utah, western Arizona, southeastern California, and northern Baja California Norte."[69] Baja California, including its northern region, is part of Mexico; given the National Forest Service information, we can deduce that Mexico is the only country outside the U.S. known to support the native growth of Joshua trees.

Despite this debunking, it should be noted that *The Joshua Tree* album title is partially attributed to Bono himself believing in the California and the Holy Land myth.

The revelation that Bono was under the impression Joshua trees could be found in Israel came from Stephen Averill, the Irish punk musician and graphic designer responsible for nearly all of U2's album cover designs; the recognizable U2 iconography designed to symbolize each of the band's eras; and, the band's very name (he maintains "It was always U2, never "*the* U2").[70] Averill was part of the crew that accompanied the band on the famed December 1986

---

68 "Joshua Tree: Evading The Jaws Of Los Angeles Greed." HuffPost.Com. *Huffington Post,* January 5, 2017. https://www.huffpost.com/entry/joshua-tree-evading-the-jaws-of-los-angeles-greed_b_585ebd6ee4b0 4d7df167cfe2.

69 "Fire Effects Information System (FEIS) - Yucca Brevifolia." fs.usda.gov. U.S. Forest Service, https://www.fs.usda.gov/database/feis/plants/tree/yucbre/all.html.

70 Averill, Stephen. "Chapter 1 - Introduction." U2-Y: A Design Story. April 28, 2023. https://podcasts.apple.com/us/podcast/chapter-1-introduction/id1685192161?i=1000611019093.

road trip through the California desert in search of landscapes that would support the "Two Americas" concept for the visual art of the album sleeve.

When recalling the trip, Averill shared that he remembered Bono being drawn to the idea that the Joshua tree only grows in two places. "When we were actually on the bus, I remember sitting with Bono and Anton (Corbijn)," Averill told the *U2-Y* podcast.

He continued, "We talked about the fact that the Joshua tree only grows in two places: in that part of the desert, and in Israel. So they saw a spiritual connection between those two things."[71]

While the idea that Joshua trees grow exclusively in California and the Holy Land is not "a fact," believing in this myth while working on *The Joshua Tree* record turned out to be fortuitous. Had Bono not believed this, there's a strong possibility that a "Two Americas" title would have stuck—and if it had, who knows how that would have impacted critical and consumer reception of the album.

Mystery: Joshua and Jesus, Bono and the Bible

Although a precise origin for the California and the Holy Land myth is unclear, one theory is that the idea took hold because of the biblicality of the name Joshua. This segues into the next mystery of *The Joshua Tree*: one involving Joshua and Jesus, which may have inspired Bono while reading the Bible.

Lusty made the case for this in her *Huffington Post* essay. "The legend probably leads back to the genesis of the name," she wrote. "When Mormons settled here for sanctuary, they named the tree Joshua because it resembled the outstretched arms of Joshua leading Israelites to glory in battle against Ai (who was consequently hung from a tree after assassination)." She also offered a simpler alternative: "Another reason could be that Joshua is Greek for [the name] Jesus, and the trees resemble Christ's outstretched arms on the cross."[72]

---

71 Averill, Stephen. "Chapter 6 - The Joshua Tree." U2-Y: A Design Story. May 29, 2023. https://podcasts.apple.com/us/podcast/chapter-6-the-joshua-tree/id1685192161?i=1000614886401.

72 "Joshua Tree: Evading The Jaws Of Los Angeles Greed." HuffPost.Com. *Huffington Post*, January 5, 2017. https://www.huffpost.com/entry/joshua-tree-evading-the-jaws-of-los-angeles-greed_b_585ebd6ee4b0 4d7df167cfe2.

As Corbijn has told it, his idea to shoot the band with one or more Joshua trees was met with Bono's enthusiasm because of the singer's devotion to the scriptures. On a 1999 episode of the VH1 series *Classic Albums*, Corbijn recalled that after he suggested the concept of shooting the band with Joshua trees, "Bono then came down [the next] morning after that night, and he came down with the Bible, and he went like, 'the Yoshua tree.' And he looked that up in the Bible, and it meant a lot to him. And he thought that should probably be a title for an album."[73]

Whether Bono was perusing references to trees in the Psalms, or reading the biblical book of Joshua itself, has never been revealed—which is why, although the Bible's influence on Bono is (lyrical humor alert) "no secret at all," his attraction to the precise spiritual symbolism of the Joshua tree remains ambiguous enough to be labeled a mystery. Plus, as a footnote, Joshua trees are not actually *in* the Bible.

Regardless, Bono—who had been determined to give this record a greater religiosity than the previous four U2 albums—evidently felt the tree supported the biblical connection he was looking for. In the band's definitive autobiography *U2 by U2*, Bono stated, "I wanted something biblical. My understanding of the scriptures were the Psalms of David and the lyricism of the King James Bible, and I tried to bring that in."[74]

Mystery: The Travelers to the Tree

The U2 canon is full of legends and lore; among the quintessential examples is the December 1986 road trip that produced the visual art of *The Joshua Tree*. According to two of the U2 associates who accompanied the band on the journey, there was a total of ten travelers in the convoy. During a recorded conversation in 2017 later released on the *U2-Y* podcast, former U2 assistant Marc Coleman recalled how the caravan that would accompany the band was assembled by tour manager Dennis Sheehan. "It was a very small crew," Coleman said. "Yes, the four band [members] were there

---

73 *Classic Albums - U2: The Joshua Tree*. VH1, 1999. https://www.dailymotion.com/video/x5nldo1.

74 McCormick, Neil, Bono, The Edge, Adam Clayton, and Larry Mullen Jr. 2006. *U2 by U2*. Harper Collins.

... there was Marion Smyth who was there, our stylist ... Anton Corbijn, the Dutch master ... his assistant Julian ... and one other guy, a guy called Steve from Windmill Lane ... And he traveled in a small jeep. Thank God we had another vehicle. And off we went!"[75]

The recorded conversation took place because Averill (the tenth member in this cast of characters) wished to speak with Coleman to commemorate the thirtieth anniversary of the record. If there is any lingering mystery surrounding who traveled with the band on *The Joshua Tree* journey through California, this reflection solves it.

Myth: The Album Cover Locations

It's the myth that won't die: the one that leads people away from, rather than closer to, the two sacred sites featured in the front and back album cover photos of *The Joshua Tree*. Despite the availability of information that has emerged over the nearly four decades since the release of the record (particularly over the last decade as the most relevant details have been published online), there are still sojourners who attempt to find both album cover locations in or near Joshua Tree National Park—despite the fact that *neither* photo was shot in the Joshua Tree area.

Why the Myth Matters: A Cautionary Tale

It's no exaggeration: If any of these myths has the potential to be perilous, it's this one. Perhaps the most cautionary tale is the story of Dutch music venue manager Guus Van Hove and his wife Helena Nuellett.

In summer 2011, the couple traveled from their home in Europe to Southern California; one of their goals for the trip was to locate and visit U2's Joshua tree. Although the source of their misinformation is not known, Van Hove and Nuellett were reportedly under the false impression that the tree was located in or near Joshua Tree National Park. Sadly, believing this myth led to their tragic deaths amid temperatures reaching 104 degrees Fahrenheit.

75 Coleman, Marc. "Bonus - Death Valley '86." U2-Y: A Design Podcast. https://podcasts.apple.com/us/podcast/bonus-death-valley-86/id1685192161?i=1000615706303.

At the time, a website for Van Hove's music venue reported that he spoke to co-workers "with a passion" about finding the tree on his trip to America.[76] He and Nuellett died on Black Eagle Mine Road, some 300 miles south of the tree's true location—a five-hour drive away. On May 20, 2017, Bono mentioned the couple by name while on stage at the Rose Bowl, saying, "We dedicate tonight's concert to Guus Van Hove and Helena Nuellett, two U2 fans. These desert songs mean a lot to us, and it seems they mean so much to you, too."[77]

At the time of the couple's death, *LA Weekly* writer Simone Wilson acknowledged the danger of the myth that led to their demise: "Though the actual location of the Joshua Tree in the photo is located some hours north, near Death Valley, it seems to be a common misconception all over the internet that the tree's namesake park hosted the shoot."[78] Roughly 3 million visitors per year visit Joshua Tree National Park safely; with proper planning and provisions, traveling into the park is generally a safe endeavor. However, attempting to find U2's Joshua tree there *is* dangerous—for the simple fact that the tree is not located there.

Fortunately, it is possible to successfully locate the two most recognizable backdrops of *The Joshua Tree*: the aforementioned tree on the back cover, and the dreamy lunar landscape on the front cover. U2 fans from all over the world have accomplished both.

For those who wish to do the same, the following information can help dispel the dangerous locational myth and inform the plans of pilgrims in search of the two sacred sites of *The Joshua Tree*. Please note that both are in the Death Valley region; adequate preparation is required for a safe journey.

---

76 Wilson, Simone. "Guus Van Hove, Dutch Music Man Who Died in Joshua Tree, May Have Been Searching for Site of U2's Album Cover." *LA Weekly*, August 25, 2011. https://www.laweekly.com/guus-van-hove-dutch-music-man-who-died-in-joshua-tree-may-have-been-searching-for-site-of-u2s-album-cover/.

77 "U2 - Rose Bowl, USA 20-May-2017 (Multicam With Enhanced Audio)." Leo U2Concerts. June 7, 2017. Video, https://www.youtube.com/watch?v=x2LXprzt4bU.

78 Wilson, Simone. "Guus Van Hove, Dutch Music Man Who Died in Joshua Tree, May Have Been Searching for Site of U2's Album Cover." *LA Weekly*, August 25, 2011. https://www.laweekly.com/guus-van-hove-dutch-music-man-who-died-in-joshua-tree-may-have-been-searching-for-site-of-u2s-album-cover/.

ZABRISKIE POINT

Exploring the Badlands

DEATH VALLEY NATIONAL PARK

Front Cover Location: Zabriskie Point

The front album cover was shot at Zabriskie Point in Death Valley National Park. The NPS promotes Zabriskie Point as an iconic Death Valley vista and a favorite location for viewing sunrise and sunset; these views are some of the most photographed in the 3,373,063 square-mile park.[79] The lookout portion of the vista, where U2 is believed to have stood for the front album cover photo, is a quarter-mile (approximately 400 meters) walk up a hill on a paved trail. The out-and-back trail is generally considered an easy route that takes an average of ten minutes to complete, according to AllTrails.com.[80] (Humorous side note: It should come as no surprise to fans that the four members of U2, cloaked in black trench coats on a wind-chilled winter's day, would likely not attempt a more difficult hike than this.) The parking lot is located east on Highway 190, fifteen minutes from the Furnace Creek Visitor Center.

Back Cover Location: The Joshua Tree, AKA "The Tree"

The once-living Joshua tree famously featured on the back cover with the band—a site known colloquially as "The Tree" to U2 fans worldwide—is also located in the Death Valley region, although not within the boundaries of Death Valley National Park. The site, which falls under the jurisdiction of the U.S. Bureau of Land Management, should only be found safely using GPS coordinates. More information to follow.

How to Obtain Location Coordinates or Driving Directions

Driving directions to the tree's precise location off Highway 190 can be obtained via trusted mapping tools, including Google Maps and iPhone's Apple Maps. Although one should exercise discernment when sourcing, some fans prefer to obtain the GPS coordinates by word of mouth from others who have previously visited. Many of these fans have passed down the information through the decades, closely guarding the numeric sequence of the coordinates due to increased online exposure. Whether one chooses

---

79 "Zabriskie Point - Death Valley National Park." nps.gov. U.S. National Park Service, https://www.nps.gov/places/zabriskie-point-scenic-viewpoint.htm

80 "Zabriskie Point." AllTrails.com. https://www.alltrails.com/trail/us/california/death-valley-national-park-zabriskie-point.

to use a technology resource or reach out to a trusted fan who has previously visited, doing the investigative groundwork to locate the coordinates before venturing out in search of the tree is critical. The coordinates are not printed here for two reasons:

1. **To preserve the site's sanctity.** At the time of this publication, the coordinates have remained a closely guarded "secret" shared among U2 fans for nearly forty years. Before the internet, they were only passed between fans anecdotally. Today, accurate driving directions can be found online via the aforementioned mapping tools.
2. **To prevent mistakes.** Including lengthy GPS coordinates in a printed publication can create a risk for the reader who may wish to use them. A reader entering them manually into a phone or vehicle GPS system may enter digits in error. This could potentially result in a dangerous misdirection.

By copying and pasting the coordinates into the reliable mapping tool of one's choice or using that mapping tool's driving directions, the journey to the tree can be simpler and safer. The parking information that follows should be considered a supplement to GPS guidance.

Parking

On Highway 190, park at Mile Marker 33.

Through the Desert on Foot

The tree is not visible from the road. The final portion of the journey is completed on foot.

After parking at the Mile Marker 33 sign and exiting the vehicle, hike for (roughly) a half-mile heading south into the desert to reach the tree. It can be easily identified by the U2-related artifacts and memorabilia that surround it.

If more formal directional assistance is desired, it is available at the Eastern Sierra Interagency Visitor Center, located at Highway 395 and SR 136 near the town of Lone Pine. The center can be reached at (760) 876-6222; as of 2025, its hours of operation were

8:30 a.m. to 4:30 p.m. daily. In order to properly assist, the visitor center staff will need to see the GPS coordinates or directions being used.

Safe Seasonal Planning

Traveling into the desert on foot can be a dangerous prospect any time of year. It is strongly recommended to avoid visiting in the heat of summer, as Death Valley temperatures can soar upwards of 120 degrees Fahrenheit. It is also important to note that while the Death Valley floor is at or below sea level, the site of the tree is roughly 4,000 feet in elevation and can be subject to extreme weather in any direction. Powerful winds and flash floods can strike the site any time of year. No matter the season, plan your trip according to weather forecasts for the region by taking into account temperatures, rainfall, mudslides, potential road closures, and other avoidable risks related to environmental impact. Pack ample water and food for the journey, and be aware that cell service coverage is insufficient throughout much of the area. The nearest fueling station/convenience store to the site is the Mobil station in Olancha, located at 601 US-395.

Reflections on the Journey

Only a few of U2's original travel companions—Averill, Coleman, and Corbijn—have publicly reflected on the finer details of their long-ago crusade to create the album art. As for the band members themselves, each of the four has only provided sporadic reflections over the years. Even during *The Joshua Tree* anniversary tours in 2017 and 2019, Bono's comments from the stage included sparse memories from the original journey. At *U2UV: Achtung Baby Live at Sphere* in 2023 and 2024, his periodic references to the band's "road trips" remained vague, as they were designed to provide a quick segue into the "put the Baby to bed" portion of the show that primarily featured songs from *Rattle & Hum*, the follow-up to *The Joshua Tree* that captured the band's experiences on the 1987 tour.

Fortunately, there is enough information out there to form a cohesive narrative. For U2 followers looking to plan their own journeys based on the most accurate information available,

190
Death Valley
LEFT TURN
1/4 MILE

We're beaten
and blown by the wind
Trampled in dust

Taken at Rose Bowl
May 2017

I'll show you a place
High on a desert plain
Where the streets have
no name

Taken on Highway 190
October 2021

By Brook W. Flag

these documented reflections from the band members and their counterparts may help (despite some factual variations in their respective firsthand accounts). What follows are published or broadcast quotes attributed to:

- Stephen Averill, album art designer and mentor
- Marc Coleman, band assistant
- Anton Corbijn, principal photographer
- U2 - Adam Clayton, Bono, Larry Mullen Jr., The Edge

On Planning & Arrival

Once tour manager Dennis Sheehan assembled the crew, U2's California voyage came together quickly. Although the road trip portion commenced in Reno, the band and crew flew into Los Angeles first.

Averill: "Marc had been given the task of being the tour manager for this particular trip ... I realized there were times when he needed some help with various things, so I took on that role."[81]

Coleman: "We found ourselves on a plane to Los Angeles, which neither of us had ever been to ... Just getting out of the plane into the warmth of LA, even in December, was stunning ..."[82]

Corbijn: "They flew into LA, and we made a sort of schedule to shoot for three days, I believe."[83]

Adam: "We traveled to Los Angeles and headed off into the Mojave Desert on a coach with Anton, Steve Averill, and a couple of crew. Off we went into the desert for a few days, staying in little motels, with Anton taking photographs. They were long days."[84]

On the Route Taken

If a consensus is to be formed from these reflections, it may be that the journey took the band from Reno, to Bodie, to Bishop, to Death

81 Averill, Stephen. "Chapter 6 - The Joshua Tree." U2-Y Podcast. May 29, 2023.

82 Coleman, Marc. "Bonus - Death Valley '86." U2-Y Podcast. June 5, 2023.

83 *Classic Albums - U2: The Joshua Tree.* VH1, 1999. https://www.dailymotion.com/video/x5nldo1.

84 McCormick, Neil, Bono, The Edge, Adam Clayton, and Larry Mullen Jr. 2006. *U2 by U2.* Harper Collins.

Valley, to the outer periphery of Joshua Tree National Park at the Harmony Motel, where it came to an end.

Averill: "Anton had visited various possible sites the previous week, and we had mapped out a route that took us from Reno, Nevada to a place called Bodie, a ghost town in the hills east of Sierra Nevada. It was a preserved national historic landmark and was bitterly cold with snow on the ground when we arrived there."[85]

Coleman: "Bodie is right on the border of California with Nevada. It's eleven-and-a-half thousand feet high … it's not a paved road. We did the Bodie shoot, we had to stay at this motel in the middle of nowhere after—we moved down to Death Valley the next day."[86]

Averill: "We drove to Bishop, about two o'clock in the morning … Checked in, woke up the next morning to this beautiful blue sky and freezing temperature. From that chilly climate, we traveled through the heat of Death Valley, to such seemingly romantic twilight roadside locations as the Harmony Motel."[87]

Edge: "We drove as far north as San Francisco, and down to Death Valley, Zabriskie Point, and loads of other little places along the way." *(It should be noted this is the only reference to San Francisco in any of the published firsthand accounts.)*[88]

On Conceiving *The Joshua Tree*

Although these accounts seemingly conflict, it is plausible that both occurred and contributed to the conception of The Joshua Tree album title and artwork.

Corbijn: "It was during the night after the first day of shooting that I went out at night with Bono, and I said, 'You know, there's a tree here that I love, and it's called the Yoshua tree. And it would be a

---

85 Averill, Stephen. "Death Valley '86." StephenAverill.Com. https://www.stephenaverill.com/death-valley-86.

86 Coleman, Marc. "Bonus - Death Valley '86." U2-Y Podcast. June 5, 2023.

87 Ibid.

88 McCormick, Neil, Bono, The Edge, Adam Clayton, and Larry Mullen Jr. 2006. *U2 by U2.* Harper Collins.

brilliant idea to have that on the front, and then the band would be on the back, like a continuation of a shot.'"[89]

Edge: "During one trek between two locations, we started talking about the different plants and asked the driver, 'What are those weird cactus things we're seeing all the time?' He said, 'They're Joshua trees.' I think it was Bono who said, 'That's a very interesting name. Let's do some photographs with some Joshua trees.'"[90]

On Pronouncing The "Yoshua" Tree

Corbijn's Dutch pronunciation of their most globally successful record title has provided the members of U2 with affectionate fodder for nearly forty years.

Adam: "He (Corbijn) would say 'Yoshua.' So we really got off on getting him to say 'Yoshua tree' back."[91]

Larry: "I remember Anton saying, 'Oh there's the Yoshua tree' ... so we stood there having our photograph taken by the Yoshua tree. We wanted to laugh, but Anton would get very upset if people laughed, or even smiled. It was all very funny, not that you'd know by the facial expressions on the album cover."[92]

Bono: "In fact, his pronunciation might've been closer to the original Hebrew, *Yeshua*—which years later, we discovered was the same name—but a different pronunciation of Jesus. We called our most popular album *The Jesus Tree*. Typical."[93]

On Finding The Joshua Tree

Corbijn selected the tree based on its uniquely solitary presence in the desert terrain visible from the highway.

Corbijn: "Then we went out that day to actually look for the tree, and amazingly enough, we found this beautiful tree ... standing

89 *Classic Albums - U2: The Joshua Tree.* VH1, 1999. https://www.dailymotion.com/video/x5nldo1

90 McCormick, Neil, Bono, The Edge, Adam Clayton, and Larry Mullen Jr. 2006. *U2 by U2.* Harper Collins.

91 *Classic Albums - U2: The Joshua Tree.* VH1, 1999. https://www.dailymotion.com/video/x5nldo1.

92 McCormick, Neil, Bono, The Edge, Adam Clayton, and Larry Mullen Jr. 2006. *U2 by U2.* Harper Collins.

93 Bono. 2022. *Surrender: 40 Songs, One Story.* Penguin Random House.

on its own, because this tree normally grows in big groups, it's incredible to find a [Joshua] tree on its own."[94]

Coleman: "We were driving on this two-lane blacktop road in the desert near Death Valley, and the next thing we hear, 'Stop ze bus, stop ze bus' … it's Anton. 'Anton, what's the problem?' He said, 'There! That's very rare.' And I said, 'What's rare?' And he said, 'It's a single Joshua tree.' And sure enough, about a mile out in the desert was like, a single Joshua tree. He said, 'They normally grow in groves! This could be the album cover.' I said, 'What do you want to do? We can't actually drive there.' He said, 'Stop the bus. Everybody off the bus. We're going to carry out, we walk out there.' So off we go…and we're about two or three hundred yards into the desert."[95]

Averill: "He was quite excited on the coach when he spotted it and asked us to stop. That was obviously fortuitous, and it just again emphasizes Anton's visual sense that he was able to spot this tree in the distance and kind of draw everybody into it."[96]

Edge: "It was all fairly spontaneous. We kept driving along the road until we saw this big, open hillside of these prehistoric-looking plants."[97]

Corbijn: "I've never seen another [Joshua] tree on its own since."[98]

Bono: "We then drove off, and I don't know if we'll ever find that Joshua Tree again."[99]

On Shooting the Photos

The cold December weather accounts for the four chilled facial expressions of the members of U2, frozen in time on the panoramic photos shot by Anton Corbijn with a Russian Horizon camera.

---

94 *Classic Albums - U2: The Joshua Tree.* VH1, 1999. https://www.dailymotion.com/video/x5nldo1

95 Coleman, Marc. "Bonus - Death Valley '86." U2-Y Podcast. June 5, 2023.

96 Averill, Stephen. "Chapter 6 - The Joshua Tree." U2-Y Podcast. May 29, 2023.

97 McCormick, Neil, Bono, The Edge, Adam Clayton, and Larry Mullen Jr. 2006. *U2 by U2.* Harper Collins.

98 *Classic Albums - U2: The Joshua Tree.* VH1, 1999. https://www.dailymotion.com/video/x5nldo1

99 "The Joshua Tree." *Propaganda* No. 5, May 1, 1987.

Averill: "It was very early in the morning … about 6 o'clock in the morning … It was absolutely beautiful, no wind whatsoever. Although it was like, zero degrees, there was no wind. So Bono says, 'Okay, this is going to look like July, take your shirts off, get your jackets off.' So they all strip down to their singlets in the freezing cold."[100]

Bono: "We discovered how cold and unforgiving the desert can be in the night—or, in the winter in the day. On the gatefold sleeve, Anton's photography captured us huddled in a cold landscape, gallantly refusing the role of actors pretending to be warm. I went the next level and posed in a singlet in six degrees—such commitment."[101]

On Bypassing Joshua Tree National Park

Because Corbijn spotted a symbolically lone Joshua tree as the bus sped through the Death Valley region and quickly determined its suitability as album sleeve art, there was no longer a need for the band's journey to include Joshua Tree National Park.

Averill: "If Anton hadn't spotted that tree, we would have gone to Joshua Tree National Park … I think we would have gotten a fantastic shoot with the strength of what Anton does anyway—and it wouldn't have been maybe quite as iconic as the tree that we found, but I think we would have gotten some very, very strong shots. Because there's such a sense of what the tree is, and what it means."[102]

Edge: "People still remember very clearly the image of us with that Joshua tree, but it wasn't, as most people thought, some sort of allusion to Gram Parsons and Joshua Tree Monument Park, which is quite close to Los Angeles … it was really just a reference to that whole desert southwest … For us, it was like a journey through this neutral ground to get to where we were going."[103]

---

100 Averill, Stephen. "Bonus - Death Valley '86." U2-Y Podcast. June 5, 2023.

101 Bono. 2022. *Surrender: 40 Songs, One Story.* Penguin Random House.

102 Averill, Stephen. "Chapter 6 - The Joshua Tree." U2-Y Podcast. May 29, 2023.

103 McCormick, Neil, Bono, The Edge, Adam Clayton, and Larry Mullen Jr. 2006. *U2 by U2.* Harper Collins.

On Experiencing the Desert

The band members and their companions have gone on record at various times to speak about the impact of their experience in the Southern California desert.

Averill: "It was genuinely spiritual to be in the desert … even in these harshest environments, there was life growing, and promise."[104]

Coleman: "Every single one of us … we were stunned by the sheer beauty … You almost felt the sense of opportunity that maybe pilgrims must have felt…There was nobody around, so it was quite a personal experience, but it was very communally shared."[105]

Adam: "When you get to Death Valley, you do wonder what was it that drove people to travel from east to west without really knowing what they were going to find on the other side. There was no guarantee they were even going to find land that was habitable, but they kept going and eventually found California."[106]

Larry: "So there we were, traveling through the Mojave Desert … standing at Zabriskie Point and realizing the magnitude and hugeness and beauty of America. That was the first time we got to see that side of America, just open spaces…it was amazing."[107]

Edge: "The purity of it … that's the thing, it's a pure, pure space, the desert."[108]

Bono: "A pilgrimage will often take you into the desert: odysseys, road trips, wanderings … It's been an enduring metaphor in the band's work. It's from a desert we look out on the world on our most famous album. American deserts like the Sonoran and the Mojave offered us *The Joshua Tree* as one of our most enduring emblems."[109]

---

104 Averill, Stephen. "Bonus - Death Valley '86." U2-Y Podcast. June 5, 2023.

105 Coleman, Marc. "Bonus - Death Valley '86." U2-Y Podcast. June 5, 2023.

106 McCormick, Neil, Bono, The Edge, Adam Clayton, and Larry Mullen Jr. 2006. *U2 by U2*. Harper Collins.

107 Ibid.

108 Ibid.

109 Bono. 2022. *Surrender: 40 Songs, One Story*. Penguin Random House.

Takeaway Travel Tips

The following reflections can help U2 followers plan their own pilgrimages in tribute to *The Joshua Tree*:

- From Averill's recollections, we can deduce that the Harmony Motel was among the final stops on the trip, if not *the* final stop—which would mean that the journey concluded just eight miles from what is now the north entrance of Joshua Tree National Park. This means that although the band did not enter the sanctioned grounds of the park, their journey essentially ended at its gateway.
- Because the crew landed in Los Angeles only to fly to Reno the next day for the road trip into the Eastern Sierras and Mojave, it seems that attempting to perfectly mimic the band's original travel route would be impractical. Unless time and resources permit, this can quickly defeat the purpose of the pilgrimage.
- With that in mind, the best way to plan a trip in tribute to *The Joshua Tree* is to map out destinations according to what is most convenient for one's point of origin. While some fans may opt to include the northernmost locations (Reno and Bodie) as well, many prefer to focus exclusively on the Death Valley area destinations included here, in addition to the Joshua Tree area locations presented in the next chapter.

Guardians of the Tree

How many U2 fans visit the Joshua tree every year is a mystery that may never be uncovered. Fortunately—more than two decades after the tree began to disintegrate in 2000—a passionate few have stepped forward to protect this sacred site for the foreseeable future.

Over the years, many fans have contributed by donating suitcases, guitars, and other items to replace the ones that are selfishly stolen by vandals; moreover, the artifacts left by fans range from small, simple flags to heavy, permanently installed plaques, the most famous of which is the "Have You Found What You're Looking For" plaque installed by Ernie Navarre in 2003.[110]

---

110 Bradley, Paul. "Meet the Superfan Who Made a Plaque Marking the Site of U2's Joshua Tree." *LA Weekly*, January 28, 2016

It would be impossible to highlight everyone who has played some part in enhancing the location. Here, we highlight two of the most active (yet perhaps least known) guardians of the Joshua tree, both of whom have devoted substantial time and resources to the restoration and preservation of this hallowed ground.

Edward Platero, thejoshuatree.earth

Edward Platero, a Canadian visual artist and filmmaker, traveled to the Mojave five times during the COVID-19 pandemic. Each time, he devoted untold hours to documenting the tree using advanced photogrammetry technology, resulting in 20,000 images. The goal of his project, thejoshuatree.earth, is to digitally preserve U2's Joshua tree as a piece of musical history through 3-D re-creation.

Using 3,937 of his 3-D photographs, Platero created a virtual reality model of the tree so that fans who will never have the opportunity to visit the physical location can virtually see the tree up close from anywhere in the world. To help viewers experience how countless U2 fans have honored the site, Platero also documented the artifacts left by fans from around the world and included them in his pristine model. Learn more at www. thejoshuatree.earth.

George, Preservationist + Guide

While visitors can clearly observe that someone has lovingly secured the remaining pieces of the disintegrating tree using power tools, anchor bolts, and liquid nails in order to slow down the process, they may not know the identity of the benevolent repairman.

His name is George, a mononymous fan who has been traveling from his home in Texas to preserve the Joshua tree for at least a decade. He has made the trip in every season of the year and every weather condition that hits the Mojave floor. Amid widespread road closures that occurred in 2024 after Hurricane Hilary delivered historic flooding to Death Valley, George continued traveling to the tree—remarkably, on mountain bike—taking a detour route of more than six miles. In addition, numerous fans who have traveled from around the world have benefited from their encounters with George while attempting to locate the tree. A playlist of videos documenting many of his missions at the site can be viewed at youtube.com/@RAMBLE_ON.

Digital Documentation: Artifacts and Notes

Together, Platero and George have worked to digitally document hundreds of artifacts left at the tree by U2 fans (including those items cast into the desert by vandals, which George has located via drone). Moreover, they have taken care to electronically scan each page of the binders on which fans have handwritten messages of devotion to the band (the closest thing to a sign-in at the site).

Their goal is to create a comprehensive digital record of the pages so that no matter the fate of the physical binders, the notes will be preserved. "I spent an entire day, sunup to sundown, inventorying the site," Platero said. Their dedication to this project should not go unnoticed by fans who care for the future of what is almost certainly U2's most sacred site—not just in California, but on the globe.

Respecting the Sanctity of the Desert

Leaving artifacts at the tree can be a meaningful experience for U2 fans. However, it should be noted that doing so does not adhere to the Leave No Trace ethos created by the U.S. Forest Service and upheld by nearly all major land management organizations. If you spend time at the tree and/or choose to leave an artifact, take steps to ensure you do not leave trash at the site. This is a small but powerful action to respect the sanctity of the desert.

Aerial photo courtesy of Edward Platero

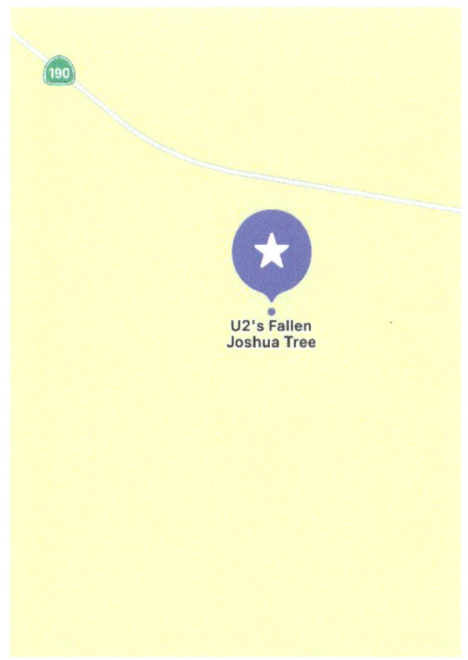

The site as shown on Apple Maps

The Joshua Tree.Earth project sign

HAVE YOU FOUND W
YOU'RE LO D FO

October 2018

Photo Credits for this Chapter

Page	Photos Contributors + Photo Dates
77	Brook W. Flagg, October 2021 Colleen Grattan, November 2021 Kevin Shannon, October 2023
92	Brook W. Flagg, October 2018
93	Brook W. Flagg, March 2019
94	Anna Conway, February 2017 Colleen Grattan, May 2017 Courtney Lavender, November 2014 & May 2018 Lisa Sloan, April 2024 Rhonda Sayers Wood, 2018
95	Monica Moser, October 2021 Christine Spencer, February 2024 Colleen Grattan, May 2017 Amanda Zimmerman, February 2025
96	Brook W. Flagg, October 2018 Mike Kurman, February 2025 Steve Follman, November 2021 Chris Phillips, June 2020 Colleen Grattan, November 2021
97	Brook W. Flagg, March 2024
98	Brook W. Flagg, March 2024
99	Brook W. Flagg, March 2024
101	Brook W. Flagg, November 2020

Surprised w/a
birthday picnic
in Joshua Tree
National Park…

the highlight of
2020

SECTION III

The
Joshua
Tree

Sites of Significance

The Joshua Tree Sites of Significance

Death Valley Junction

Location: Intersection of Hwy 190 & Hwy 127, Amargosa Valley

Significance: Full band photos in front of water towers before exiting Death Valley

Date in U2 history: (Likely) December 15, 1986

Still in operation/visitable? Yes

Crowbar Cafe & Saloon

Location: Old State Hwy 127, Shoshone Village

Significance: Patronized by the band before exiting Death Valley

Date in U2 history: (Likely) December 15, 1986

Still in operation/visitable? Yes, with patronage

Harmony Motel

Location: 71161 29 Palms Highway, Twentynine Palms

Significance: Only documented roadside motel establishment from *The Joshua Tree* excursion; final stop on the journey; only location visited by the band near Joshua Tree National Park

Date in U2 history: (Likely) night of December 15–day of December 16, 1986

Still in operation/visitable? Yes, with patronage

Joshua Tree Visitor Center

Location: 6554 Park Boulevard, Joshua Tree

Significance: Site of the only U.S. National Park Service exhibit featuring U2; one of only two Sites of Significance near Joshua Tree National Park

Still in operation/visitable? Yes

For those who wish to make the comprehensive U2 pilgrimage across the Mojave Desert, there are several sites of significance near *both* of its national parks.

Near Death Valley National Park

There are two sites rounding out U2's time in the Death Valley region. Although not much is known about their brief stops at either site, both are confirmed to be visited by the U2 caravan—one by photos, the other by reliable anecdote.

Death Valley Junction

At the eastern access point into Death Valley, Death Valley Junction teeters on the threshold of ghost town territory. The area is primarily occupied by the Amargosa Opera House (which seems like an ideal site for a Corbijn photoshoot, and yet no photos of U2 at the location have ever surfaced). Instead, Corbijn shot the band a few steps across Highway 127 in front of the two water towers that once serviced the mining operations around the Death Valley Railroad. These photos were used for multiple purposes, most notably the art for the single release of "In God's Country" and the program for *The Joshua Tree* tour.

Fans can recreate the photos (as pictured), but due to fencing that restricts access to the towers, it must be done from a much further distance than where the members of U2 stood.

Due to copyright restrictions, Corbijn's photos are not featured here; they can be found online for comparison purposes.

DEATH VALLEY JUNCTION

Crowbar Cafe & Saloon

One mile from the southeast entrance of Death Valley National Park sits Shoshone Village, a town with the only restaurant for fifty-seven miles, the Crowbar Cafe & Saloon, where U2 stopped for beers and a round of pool.

The restaurant is owned by Susan Sorrells, a great-grandchild of Shoshone founder R.J. Fairbanks. Proclaimed "Queen of the Desert" in 2022 by a compelling *New Yorker* profile, Sorrells has maintained a charming vibe at the Crowbar amid her

Discovery at the Crowbar

transformation of Shoshone Village into an eco-conscious tourism destination.[111] There are no known photos of U2 at the location—but in 2025, this book's author discovered (on a second trip there) that a framed collage of *The Joshua Tree* photos had been hung on a back wall of the restaurant. Upon further investigation, it was revealed that the photos were supplied by Jeff Fairbanks, a cousin of Sorrells and U2 fan. He kindly shared the following anecdote: "In December 1986, U2 stopped at the Crowbar, where they played pool and had some pints. The pool table used to be right by where the collage is. Susan was actually working there when the lads from Ireland stopped by." For this reason, a meal or a drink at the Crowbar is the perfect way to start or end a U2 pilgrimage in Death Valley.

---

111 Ross, Alex. "The Queen of the Desert." *The New Yorker,* January 4, 2022.

On back wall
(from 1987 tour program)

THE JOSHUA TREE

Crowbar Cafe &
Saloon 2025

Near Joshua Tree National Park

Despite the reality that the front and back covers of *The Joshua Tree* were photographed in the northern Mojave and Death Valley National Park, two sites on the southern end of the Mojave near Joshua Tree National Park can be incorporated into a U2 road trip. One of these sites was famously on the band's original desert sojourn.

Before we discuss them, let's address why the band's caravan avoided the proper boundaries of Joshua Tree National Park. At least one member of U2 has stated that the original intention *was* to shoot the band inside it. "[Corbijn] was very keen to take us to Joshua Tree Park," Adam Clayton told VH1 in 1999.[112]

Corbijn had prior experience shooting in the park with another client, the enigmatic musician Captain Beefheart. That shoot occurred seven years prior, according to a conversation between Steven Averill and his son Gareth on the *U2-Y* podcast. "It's really fascinating to look back at those images from 1980 of Captain Beefheart," Averill said. "He looks at home in the desert, like he is being photographed in his place—whereas U2 is being photographed as wayfaring strangers in a new land ... obviously, this was a powerful place for Anton to want to go back there."[113]

And yet, it seems that by the time the U2 caravan had crossed the Mojave from Death Valley to Joshua Tree, Corbijn had determined an adequate volume of visuals had been gathered for the album art—well, almost.

Harmony Motel

For fans looking to sleep where U2 slept on the periphery of Joshua Tree National Park, checking in at the Harmony Motel—where the band stayed for the final night of the trip—can certainly enhance the experience. Located at 71161 Twentynine Palms Highway, the property often called "the Harmony" is the only roadside inn from *The Joshua Tree* journey that is known by name to the U2 audience.

---

112 *Classic Albums - U2: The Joshua Tree.* VH1, 1999. https://www.dailymotion.com/video/x5nldo1.

113 Averill, Stephen. "Chapter 6 - The Joshua Tree." U2-Y: A Design Story. May 29, 2023. https://podcasts.apple.com/us/podcast/chapter-6-the-joshua-tree/id1685192161?i=1000614886401.

This knowledge is made possible because of the photos Corbijn shot there, which feature a recognizably red-lettered sign bearing the motel's name. They were included in the original album sleeve art and used again three decades later, when an image featuring each band member's individual pose in front of the motel sign was used again as a T-shirt print for *The Joshua Tree 2017* tour merchandise.

Long before a 2017 *Los Angeles Daily News* story declared the Harmony Motel "another popular spot for [U2] fan pilgrimages," faithful followers had already begun descending on the site to sleep where the band slept.[114] When Nalini "Ash" Maharaj acquired the property in 2004, she immediately embraced the strong interest from the U2 fan base. After more than two decades of ownership, she still frequently markets the motel as a U2 destination with quippy taglines like, "If U2 stayed at the Harmony, then why not 'U2'?"[115]

Thanks to her efforts, fans from around the world know they are welcome to visit the Harmony as part of a U2 pilgrimage. Some—like this author and her tight-knit group of "U2 Sisters"—stay at the Harmony the night before a trip to the sacred tree site in order to cover the entire length of the Mojave traveled by the band. Other fans may wait until U2 is on tour, opting to book a room at the Harmony before or after the band's show in Los Angeles or Las Vegas (doing this requires planning for travel times, as the 142-mile drive from Los Angeles to Twentynine Palms is roughly two-and-a-half hours; the 184-mile distance to Las Vegas means a drive just minutes shy of three hours).[116]

In addition to the outdoor sign, fans have posed for pictures with the framed Corbijn photos and U2 newspaper clippings in the motel's lobby. Previous ownership is believed to have been the source of the lore that "Bono stayed in Room Four," a legend that has made the room a popular choice for fans booking a night. Larger groups may be more comfortable in the Harmonic House, a

114 Ghori, Imran. "5 Cool Facts about U2'S 'The Joshua Tree' on Its 30 Anniversary." *Los Angeles Daily News*, August 28, 2017.

115 "IF U2 STAYED AT THE HARMONY, THEN WHY NOT U2? - the History of an Authentic Desert Getaway." HarmonyMotel.Com. https://www.harmonymotel.com/history-of-harmony-motel/.

116 "Harmony Motel and Joshua Tree." Reddit.Com. https://www.reddit.com/r/U2Band/comments/1bg5ef3/harmony_motel_and_joshua_tree/

freestanding house on the Harmony property which accommodates up to five guests and features an original Corbijn photo of the sacred tree on its living room wall. The Harmony Motel is eight miles from the north entrance of Joshua Tree National Park and eleven miles from the next site on our list, the Joshua Tree Visitor Center.

Joshua Tree Visitor Center

Although the band never entered the park on the journey, U2's connection to the region has nonetheless been formally acknowledged by Joshua Tree National Park. Inside the Joshua Tree Visitor Center at 6554 Park Boulevard (also known as the "west entrance" visitor center five miles from the park), the band is featured in a permanent exhibit paying tribute to the region's inspiration on twentieth-century musicians. *The Joshua Tree* album is displayed behind a glass case, along with a caveat informing visitors that the cover was actually shot in Death Valley. This may be a safety effort to dispel the aforementioned locational myth; regardless, it provides U2 fans a touchpoint when visiting Joshua Tree National Park. Also featured in the exhibit is the Adam Clayton quote, "The desert was immensely inspirational to us as a mental image for this record."[117]

This exhibit is the only National Park Service acknowledgment of U2's connection to the Mojave. It provides an added incentive for fans to visit both Joshua Tree and Death Valley on a U2 excursion across the desert.

---

117 Stokes, Niall . 1996. *To The Heart: The Stories Behind Every U2 Song.* Harper Collins.

Photos and art for this chapter by Brook W. Flagg.

Featured in photos for this chapter (alphabetically by last name):
Novelle Best, Brook W. Flagg, Soledad Rojas Guitierrez, Noemi Kuznicki,
Baldemar Rodriguez, Kathrin Van Gilder, Joanne Vega, Wendy Ufford

Scenes from Harmonic House

WELCOME TO JOSHUA TREE

Fresno
Visalia
Death Valley National Park
Las Vegas
Bakersfield
3 hr 51 min Fastest
5 hr 7 min
Lancaster
Mojave N Preserve
3 hr 52 min Fewer turns
os Angeles
Anaheim
Joshua Tree National Pa

Trip route across the Mojave

Brook   Soledad

PEACE

U2

BONO

U2

All I Want Is You

Babe it may be art

U2

Together again

Sisters Together again

Kathrin   Novelle

Art created at Harmonic House

2024

2019

2020

... sicians come to the desert for solitude and inspiration. The tree on the back cover of U2's album *The Joshua Tree* was photographed near Death Valley National Park.

at Joshua Tree Visitor Center

harmony JJ MOTEL

harmony JJ MOTEL

1986

2024

Harmony music room

harmony JJ MOTEL

2019

'The desert was immensely inspirati... to us as a mental image for this rec...

–Adam Clayton, bass player for U2, about *The Joshua Tree* album

at Joshua Tree N...

Visitor Center

Joshua Tree NP 2020

The Tree
(on the Harmonic
House wall)

SECTION IV

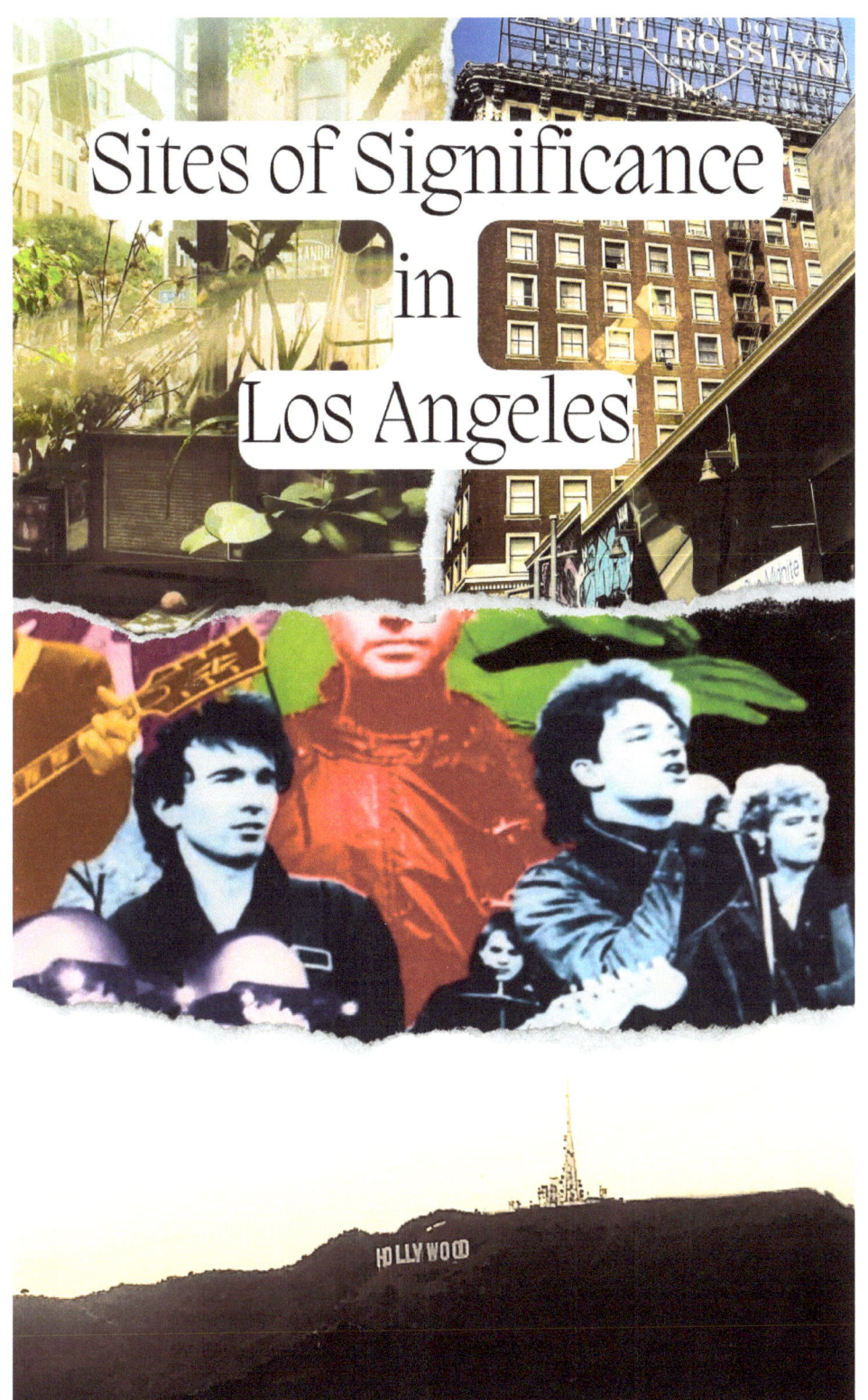

Sites of Significance in Los Angeles

U2 at Barney's Beanery
Essay by Bill See

It was late May 1988. A lazy Sunday morning, and I needed to get something in my stomach after a night of frivolity. I did a quick scroll through my brain for breakfast spots before settling on Barney's Beanery, the venerable restaurant-bar on what was once Route 66, now Santa Monica Boulevard, in West Hollywood.

Barney's had been a regular haunt for Hollywood actors like Clark Gable, Errol Flynn, and Judy Garland until the 60s when it became a hangout for hippies, musicians and poets. In the 70s TV show *Columbo*, Peter Falk often ordered chili from Barney's, and Barney's is featured in the opening credits to *Grease*. Then in the 80s, with its proximity to the Sunset Strip, it became a hangout for a combination of hip young actors and the glam/metal crowd.

I took a seat in a small booth close to the bar where Janis Joplin had her last drink and Jim Morrison once famously rose from his stool and peed on the spot, earning him a quick eighty-six. I scanned the extensive menu printed on colorful newsprint, feeling overwhelmed by the choices. The waitress, a dead ringer for Rosie the Riveter—even had her hair tied up by the same red and white polka dot bandana—asked me what I wanted while impatiently tapping her pencil against her hip. I finally ordered huevos rancheros and a coffee. I watched Rosie take my order to the kitchen, then return a minute later setting down a giant burger and fries for the B-actor type at the table across from me. I immediately regretted my order.

Faced toward the entrance, I watched four figures shuffle in, their faces silhouetted by backlit morning sun. The four crowded into the booth closest to the front the door and as they settled in, their faces became illuminated—faces I'd seen hundreds, maybe thousands of times. But other than the time I was front row at the Forum for the second date on the 1986 Amnesty International show, never *so* close. Unmistakably, sitting there from left to right were Adam, Larry, Edge, and Bono—notably with no handlers, no security, and no Paul McGuinness. Just the four of them now faced right at me, looking exactly like U2 has looked during the last meteoric year that catapulted the biggest cult band in the world to superstardom: in disheveled, quasi western garb—Edge and Bono in black hats, Adam and Larry without.

It was not surprising to see U2 at Barney's Beanery. They'd been in town since February, working with Phil Joanou to finish off the film they'd started during the last leg of *The Joshua Tree* tour last fall. And it was rumored they were recording new songs with Jimmy Iovine, just a mile away at A&M Studios. Barney's, along with the Formosa just up Santa Monica Boulevard and the Flaming Colossus in downtown LA, were U2's favorite watering holes since they'd been in town. Plus, the Sunset Marquis hotel where the band has stayed since the *Boy* tour was just steps away.

But while I'd been a massive U2 fan from day one, I wasn't a meet-my-heroes kind of guy. Maybe I was scared after waiting at the back entrance of the Sports Arena for The Who to come out after their show in 1980, hoping to tell Pete Townshend he saved my life. Four limos with tinted windows raced up the ramp and peeled away, ending that hope.

So, I figured it was best to just love and admire from afar.

The only time I'd ever actually felt comfortable talking to anyone famous was when I was in an elevator with Sidney Poitier, and that was only because we were all alone for a precious fifteen seconds. I sheepishly put out my hand and offered, "Mr. Poitier, I don't mean to bother you, but I'm a great admirer of your work."

I'd wasted ten seconds trying to convince myself to talk to him—so by the time he reacted, the doors were opening. He turned, said, "Thank you, young man," and left.

So, sitting there at Barney's with a half-eaten plate of huevos rancheros in front of me, I had no plans to get up and bother U2's meal. *But*, I thought to myself, *isn't this interesting*. U2 was, without exaggeration, at that moment, the biggest band in the world. *The Joshua Tree* had become one of those records that soccer moms had; lawyers and doctors and insurance guys hummed their songs in traffic. It was no longer the fanzines that covered them, but *Entertainment Tonight* and *People* magazine.

But there they were, on a quiet Sunday morning. Just the four of them, talking, laughing, taking the piss. It wasn't hard to realize what a serene moment that must have been for them. No one pulling at them. Asking for autographs. Being whisked away for another interview or show. They just looked like the four mates they always said they were. There was something strangely comforting about that, which was why I was torn. I mean, if there was ever a time to meet them, this was it. But why risk it, right? Why ruin that perfect moment that had already been imprinted in my brain and assigned a special place in a safe box in my memory?

But then, Edge looked up and right at me, and smiled before going back to nursing his coffee. I kind of reflexively took a look behind me—like, "Oh, you talking to that invisible guy back there?" But there really was no one else in the joint but me and the B-movie guy whose name I couldn't remember.

After Rosie cleared my table and left me the bill, I sat there, replaying in my mind all the seminal moments I'd shared with U2. "Shared." Funny, right? Well, we *were* sharing the same space. The Hollywood Palladium, Long Beach Arena, the Sports Arena, the Forum. And I thought about that morning I sat alone on the green shag carpet of my living room, watching Live Aid right after my grandfather died and my mom was battling her demons. The way I felt watching Bono leap from the stage for a connecting moment. Somehow through the satellite waves, it reached me, and I felt just a little less alone.

I got up to pay the bill, trying to think of something to say that wouldn't sound like a fanboy … something that wouldn't take too long to get out of my mouth … something that wouldn't require them to even answer. I guess I just didn't want to ruin the moment (for them. Or that picture I had of them, if I'm being honest). I paid the bill and realized there was no other way to exit. Their table was right by the front door. As I got closer, I made up my mind I wasn't going to bother them. And I was fine with that. But Edge's eyes turned to me as I approached, and I felt myself slow down as I was pulled by a force beyond myself. As much as I can remember—though I'll confess, it's always been a little fuzzy—I leaned over, ever so, and said, "I don't mean to bug you …"

I'm kidding. Bono's line from *Rattle & Hum* hadn't come out yet. Seriously, I said to no one in particular (though Larry was in the middle, so I probably was staring generally at him): "I just wanted to pay a debt of gratitude. It was The Who, The  Clash, then U2. I don't think I would've made it without you." And I walked away.

"Streets" Video Site at 7th & Main

Location: Intersection of 7th and Main Streets, Los Angeles
Significance: Rooftop site of the "Where the Streets Have No Name" video shoot
Date in U2 history: March 27, 1987
Still in operation/visitable? Yes

"The object was to close down the streets. If there's one thing people in LA hate, it's streets closing down, and we've always felt bands should shake things up. We achieved it because the police stopped us [from] filming. Were we worried about being arrested? Not at the time."
— Adam Clayton, Q magazine, 2010[118]

March 27, 1987 would not be the last time U2 attempted an innovative stunt for greater visibility, but it's arguably one of the most memorable. In the decades since the band ascended the rooftop of the Republic Liquor Store at the corner of 7th and Main Streets to perform for a crowd of onlookers and fans who assembled that afternoon as cameras were rolling, reflections of the event have been broadly nostalgic and positive, yet cautiously so ("carefully planned chaos," declared *The Globe and Mail* in 2017, but "not quite as impromptu as it appeared," said *LAist* in 2013).[119]

The Biggest Chapter Yet

The idea to shoot a guerrilla-style video for the third single from *The Joshua Tree* was inspired by the Beatles' impromptu rooftop performance on January 30, 1969, atop their Apple Corps headquarters in London.

Despite Bono's quip "It's not the first time we ripped off the Beatles," U2 was aware the two performances would differ in

---

118 Knolle, Sharon. "Flashback Monday: U2 Performs On A Roof In Downtown L.A." *LAist*, September 22, 2013. https://laist.com/news/flashback-monday-u2-performs-on-a-r.

119 Lederman, Marsha. "Carefully Planned Chaos: A Look at how an Iconic Video Came Together 30 Years Ago." *The Globe and Mail*, May 9, 2017; Ibid.

multiple ways.[120] For one thing, the Beatles' rooftop performance turned out to be the *last* Beatles performance. For another, the Apple Corps building was situated at 3 Savile Row in London's fashion district—whereas the members of U2 would hold their performance on a block that is, quite literally, at the gateway to LA's Skid Row. The juxtaposition spoke for itself, and U2 wanted the world to hear it.

The approximately seven-minute "Streets" video was directed by Meiert Avis, who had previously directed six other videos for the band. Just one month prior, they shot the video for the previous single, "With or Without You," in Dublin.

Although "Streets" would be the third single off *The Joshua Tree*, its video shoot took place before that of the second single, "I Still Haven't Found What I'm Looking For," which was famously shot on Fremont Street in Las Vegas the night of April 12, right after the band played the Thomas and Mack Arena—the first-ever U2 concert in Las Vegas.[121]

Although the two aforementioned videos were released before "Streets," the song's video had to represent—at least from the standpoint of U2, its management, and the video's director—a new chapter and breakthrough for the band. Despite having toured the States many times over at that point to promote the previous four studio albums, U2 was still frequently portrayed as a quaint Irish import, even by the standards of MTV and the radio stations that gave them airplay. If *The Joshua Tree* was to be different—that is, if it was to fill the extraordinarily tall order of solidifying U2's reputation as part of the new rock n roll establishment while simultaneously catapulting the band into global superstardom—then the public image of the band had to start evolving from the first notes of the album. Those notes are heard in "Streets," the seminal first track of *The Joshua Tree.*

As the album release date drew near in March 1987, Avis traveled to LA and began making arrangements for a video shoot that would announce the biggest U2 chapter yet. The

120 Eskin, Marah. "U2 Took Over Downtown L.A. for 'Where the Streets Have No Name.'" *Ultimate Classic Rock*. March 22, 2022. https://ultimateclassicrock.com/u2-where-the-streets-have-no-name-video/.

121 "U2 Joshua Tree Tour The Joshua Tree 1st Leg: North America 1987-04-12: Thomas And Mack Arena - Las Vegas, Nevada, USA." U2gigs.Com. https://www.u2gigs.com/show266.html.

announcement was not the video; the announcement was the video *shoot*, designed to attract widespread media attention. As director of the iconic video, Avis went on record years later to say as much. Thirty years after the video was filmed—on the eve of the band's first night of *The Joshua Tree 2017* tour in Vancouver, no less—Avis, who now resides in LA, told Canada's *The Globe and Mail* the point of staging that long-ago downtown rooftop performance on a busy Friday afternoon was "to be disruptive, the truth be told ... That was the album that was going to put them into the public eye, so [we were] using a flash mob scenario to create a spontaneous media event that one couldn't help but notice."[122]

As explained by Marsha Lederman for *The Globe and Mail*, "The stunt was also meant to announce U2's arrival to the big, big time. U2—a band Avis had been working with since the beginning—were already rock stars, but with the release of *The Joshua Tree*, they were on the brink of being gigantic."[123]

In the end, the mission would be accomplished. But as the shoot got underway, no one could be certain of the final result. There were challenges galore—chief among them, the location.

"Not one of the most delightful neighborhoods"

Like all official U2 music videos, the "Streets" video can easily be found online, including on YouTube. As the video opens, local DJs and newscasters can be heard announcing the "surprise" performance/video shoot that would take place that day at the corner of 7th and Main Streets.

"7th and Main Street's not one of your more fun neighborhoods," one says.

"Use caution if you do go down there," says another, "because it is, like, not one of the most delightful neighborhoods." The warning came from DJ Rita Wilde, who was then an announcer at KLOS 95.5 FM.

Keith Morrison, now better known as a host on *Dateline NBC*, was a local reporter for NBC4 Los Angeles in the late 80s. Among

---

122 Lederman, Marsha. "Carefully Planned Chaos: A Look at how an Iconic Video Came Together 30 Years Ago." *The Globe and Mail*, May 9, 2017.

123 Ibid.

the local reporters whose comments were included in the video's opening seconds, the most recognizable voice is his. "I'm not making this up! 3:30 today, 7th and Main," Morrison says in a manner that might now be considered uncharacteristic of his distinctively low, silky tone. "I'm gonna be there, 3:30! I'm gonna go over there, I don't care. I can be sucked into this. I'll be in the video!"[124]

From the crowd of thousands, those who can be seen in the final product include fist-pumping young men hanging off of street fixtures; an elderly woman pushing a tiny dog in a stroller; and a breakdancer whose every move is somehow synching with the music. Some in the crowd were U2 fans, while many were simply the residents and business owners who could be found walking that block on any given day. While the number 30,000 has been used to describe the expected crowd attendance, time has tempered the estimate substantially. "The performance attracted about 1,000 people, not the 30,000 predicted in the radio clips at the beginning of the video," wrote Sharon Knolle for *LAist*.[125]

Sunlight on My Face

To experience the "Streets" video as somatically as possible, one should consider the season in which it was shot—but only after first considering the season that preceded it. Five months before U2 shot the video with Meiert Avis, the band members were captured by Anton Corbijn amid an ice cold wind chill near Death Valley. The album sleeve art that depicted them stripped of their outer clothing as they surrounded the newly discovered Joshua tree was intended to evoke the idea of having braved the Mojave Desert heat to find it—when in reality, it was found in December. Standing in the remote location off Highway 190 ten days before the onset of winter solstice, all four band members visibly struggled to hide the sting of the ice cold air on their faces. Considering this reality while hearing the lyrics "blown by the wind" and "high on a desert plain" delivers

124 "U2 - Where The Streets Have No Name (Official Music Video)." U2. December 14, 2009. Video, https://www.youtube.com/watch?v=GzZWSrr5wFI&list=RDGzZWSrr5wFI&start_radio=1.

125 Knolle, Sharon. "Flashback Monday: U2 Performs On A Roof In Downtown L.A." *LAist*, September 22, 2013. https://laist.com/news/flashback-monday-u2-performs-on-a-r.

a powerful winter blast to the listening ear (and visiting the sacred site of the tree in winter drives it home all the more).

Fast forward five months to March 1987, when Meiert Avis shot the video for the same song. This time, U2 would be captured playing with joyful intention on a downtown Los Angeles rooftop on one of the first days of spring. For more than seven minutes, the four members are seen frolicking on a promising Friday afternoon while the sun's rays flicker and glint on film. It's everything people love about an early spring day—especially in Southern California, where the idea of "seasonal weather" can be an unpredictable oxymoron. Every frame of the video featuring a member of the band embodies the hopefulness of the lyric "I wanna feel sunlight on my face." As Avis has told it, "The whole thing was meant to happen in magic hour as the sun went down." When shooting began, sunset was still three hours away—but it seems magic hour began early that day.

A rewatch of the video depicts the band members playing the respective character roles they remain recognized for to this day. We see Adam Clayton resembling a shirtless spring breaker, bass in hand, grooving in the signature style he has maintained over the decades. We see a top-hatted Edge, ever the orchestrator, bustling about the roof as if checking to make sure all is going as planned. We see Larry clothed in a tight motorcycle graphic tee, pounding away with the intensity and fervor that has since become his trademark as a drummer. And we see a flowing-haired, button-downed Bono—wistful, windswept, and (quite ironically) the only member of U2 who was *not* protecting his eyes with shades on that sun-drenched day. He sang "Streets" a total of four times, so the story goes; also played were "People Get Ready," "In God's Country," "Sunday Bloody Sunday," and "Pride (In the Name Of Love)." And although the dramatic police shutdown shown in the video was technically real, that was all part of the plan.[126]

---

126 Eskin, Marah. "U2 Took Over Downtown L.A. for 'Where the Streets Have No Name.'" *Ultimate Classic Rock.* March 22, 2022. https://ultimateclassicrock.com/u2-where-the-streets-have-no-name-video/.

"I think [the police] behaved impeccably, frankly," Avis recalled. "They didn't lose their marbles, they didn't get angry, but they were totally firm. Eventually, they pulled the fuse out of the generator."[127]

The new chapter of U2 began with a bang, and people took notice. According to Avis, he and the band decamped to their hotel after the shoot to eagerly watch themselves on the news. That hotel, the Sunset Marquis, had long been U2's home away from home in LA and would later be the site of a tragedy that struck the heart of the band (this will be explored in the next site entry). In March 1987, the Sunset Marquis was home base for the activities surrounding the album release, including the shoot for one of the most beloved videos in U2 history. Although "Streets" would peak at number thirteen on the U.S. *Billboard* Hot 100, the video won U2 and Meiert Avis, along with producers Ben Dossett and Michael Hamlyn, the Best Performance Music Video trophy at the 31st Annual Grammy Awards. The fact that it was awarded almost two years later in February 1989 speaks to the lasting impression the "Streets" video made on everyone from music consumers to industry peers.

The video announced the biggest chapter of U2 yet, ushered the band into the new establishment, and achieved global super-stardom. It was a tall order, but "Streets" did it in a way that inspired countless music videos by other artists for decades to come.

From Sunset to Streets

In 1987, Ryan Carroll was a 20-year-old student at El Camino College in Torrance. He recalled a general protocol music fans would follow if they wanted to catch a glimpse of (much less meet) their heroes, remembered so fondly that he recalled it in the present tense. "Whenever the band you like is in town," he said, "first and foremost you go to the Sunset Marquis. After that, you go to the Hyatt House—the Riot House, they called it. And then Chateau Marmont. One of those three. And in the 80s, U2 was always at the Sunset Marquis." One of his most memorable encounters with U2 happened March 27, 1987, a day that started like any other Friday en route to

---

127 Lederman, Marsha. "Carefully Planned Chaos: A Look at how an Iconic Video Came Together 30 Years Ago." *The Globe and Mail*, May 9, 2017.

class. It began at the Sunset Marquis, but ended at one of the most significant U2 sites in Los Angeles: 7th and Main.

"On my way to school," Carroll recalled, "Richard Blade on KROQ says what's going to go down in LA that morning." His best friend since grade school, Scott Middleman, had just arrived at the college as Carroll was pulling his car into the lot. "I park next to Scott and he hears the same. 'Dude, did you hear what was on KROQ this morning? U2's shooting a video. Let's go.'"

So they did. "No brainer, I jump in his car and we're off," he said. "We knew if U2 was in town, they're gonna be at the Sunset Marquis." The drive from El Camino College to the hotel is about twenty-four miles to the north. It's roughly forty minutes, without traffic (even in 1987, LA traffic was still LA traffic). When the two friends arrived, they saw all four members of U2—but the meeting didn't happen yet, as the band was quickly piling into two cars. Fortunately, the story didn't end there; the adventure continued, and it placed these two fans in the center of U2's most historic LA story to date.

"Sure enough, as soon as we get there, Bono, Adam, and Larry are piling into a Toyota. Edge got in a different car. A Buick Regal, I think. We follow them from there, and both cars stop across the street from Guitar Center on Sunset."

It's another "this could never happen today" story: two best friends meet their favorite band on the Sunset Strip. As Edge signed an instrument inside Guitar Center, Carroll and Middleman got autographs from Bono, Adam and Larry in the college notebooks they had on them after skipping school to follow the band. When Edge returned to the Buick and it took off, the two fans followed them—all the way to 7th and Main, where they were among the crowd who made it into the "Streets" video.

The "Streets" Site Today

Today, the Republic Liquor store is Margarita's Place, a small restaurant that also occupied the liquor store space in 1987 (as indicated in photos of the video shoot, which show Margarita's Place signage on the south side of the building). U2 fans over the decades who have asked the restaurant for roof access have been consistently denied—so while ordering a burrito and taking a picture in view of the street corner is recommended, asking the management to let you climb onto their roof is not.

"The Million Dollar Hotel" Nearby

The Hotel Rosslyn, known for its massive sign proclaiming it to be the "New Million Dollar Hotel Rosslyn," is located just two blocks east at 5th and Main. All four members of U2 spent time at the hotel while they lived in LA to record tracks for *Rattle & Hum*; these visits famously inspired Bono's screenplay "The Million Dollar Hotel," which was brought to life in the 2000 Wim Wenders film of the same name starring Mel Gibson, Milla Jovovich, and Jeremy Davies.

"The Million Dollar Hotel" premiered at the 50th Berlin Film Festival in February 2000 with Bono in attendance. At the screening, he reflected on the band's long-ago encounters at the hotel. "I visited there in the late 80s and couldn't quite believe my eyes," Bono said. "In every room, there was a story—all these characters living in downtown LA in this, you know, kind of halfway house hotel … good people, bad people, pimps, hookers, mothers with lots of children … It's just looking at them thinking (how) this is in the middle of Los Angeles, this hotel with its, you know, sea of marble in the 30s, in the Golden Era of Hollywood … It was the palace, and here it is now."[128]

Unfortunately, despite its close proximity to the site of the "Streets" shoot, visiting the Rosslyn is no longer a safe proposition. The hotel has been converted into a Skid Row residential property, and is therefore not a recommended destination for U2 fans.[129] The next best option for those who wish to see it is to carefully take a photo of the "New Million Dollar Hotel" sign from a safe distance.

128 "Bono (U2) about Movie The Million Dollar Hotel: 'I Visited The Actual Hotel' | Interview | TMF." TMF - The Music Factory. August 17, 2023. Video, https://www.youtube.com/watch?v=WeLQxGZS3T8.

129 Zassenhaus, Eric. "Downtown LA's Historic Rosslyn Hotel Apartments Set to Become Permanent Housing for Homeless.", June 26, 2014. https://laist.com/news/kpcc-archive/rosslyn-apartments-downtown-los-angeles-homeless.

7th & Main

1987

WHERE THE STREETS HAVE NO NAME

U2

2022

NEW MILLION DOLLAR
1100
HOTEL ROSSLYN
FIRE
ROOMS
PROOF
POPULAR
PRICES

Sites of Significance on the Sunset Strip

Sunset Marquis

Location: 1200 Alta Loma Road, West Hollywood

Significance: Historic hotel for musical artists; early U2's Los Angeles "home"; site of tour manager Dennis Sheehan's passing

Dates in U2 history: Various, 1981–2015

Still in operation/visitable? Yes, with patronage

Chateau Marmont

Location: 8221 W Sunset Blvd., Los Angeles, CA 90046

Significance: Historic hotel; U2's second hotel preference

Dates in U2 history: Various, 90s–2000s

Still in operation/visitable? Yes, with patronage

Book Soup

Location: 8818 W Sunset Blvd., West Hollywood, CA 90069

Significance: Inspiration resource for *The Joshua Tree* aesthetic; vendor chosen to distribute Bono's *Surrender: 40 Songs, One Story* to Los Angeles *Stories of Surrender* attendees

Dates in U2 history: Various, 1986–2022

Still in operation/visitable? Yes, with patronage

"LA is a strange place. As long as you think it's strange, then you're all right. I think it's strange, and I'm pretty damn strange too."[130]

– Bono, *SPIN magazine*, 1989

---

130 Staff, SPIN. "U2: Our 1989 Cover Story." *SPIN* Magazine, November 2, 2019.
   https://www.spin.com/featured/u2-bono-rattle-and-hum-january-1989-cover-story-hating/.

Sunset Boulevard has remained an emblematic beacon of LA culture (and counterculture) for more than one hundred years. The street's most famous stretch of road, the 1.7 miles known as the Sunset Strip, holds decades of musical lore. The Strip's reputation is storied as a breeding ground for American glam rock and a decadent playground for iconic British acts that are now household names: Page, Plant, Jagger, and John (as in Elton). But Sunset has a place in U2 history as well—several places, in fact. The band has spent time at some of its most enduring West Hollywood destinations, from the novel to the seminal.

"... Even Tower Records on the Sunset Strip was made famous for its gigantic album covers promoting the music of the day. The whole city felt young and of the moment."[131]

– Bono, *Surrender: 40 Songs, One Story*, 2022

Staying at the Sunset Marquis

The Sunset Marquis, located a quick turn off the Strip at 1200 Alta Loma Road, has been a renowned retreat for musicians and other artists for the majority of its existence. When George Rosenthal founded the hotel in 1963, he designed it to emulate the Garden of Allah, a mansion-turned-hotel that was demolished four years prior. Rosenthal described his vision as "a regeneration of what I'd only read about: a wonderful gathering place for the exchange of ideas for writers, musicians, people in the film business."[132]

In a few years, that vision would materialize. The earliest days of hotel operations overlapped with the opening of the Whisky a Go Go in 1964—and by the 70s, the Sunset Marquis was known as a getaway for musicians looking for a reprieve from the groupie culture that had infested other hotels on the Strip (specifically the Sunset Boulevard Hyatt, also known as the "Hyatt House"). The absence of groupies made the Sunset Marquis a natural fit for a

---

131 Bono. 2022. *Surrender: 40 Songs, One Story*. Penguin Random House.

132 "If These Walls Could Rock History: 50 Years and Counting at the Sunset Marquis." SunsetMarquis.Com. https://sunsetmarquis.com/about-west-hollywood-hotel/history/.

young U2; as Andy Greene wrote for *Rolling Stone* in 2014, "U2 were never a band with much of a reputation for bagging groupies."[133]

Evidence points to the band members' initial naïveté about the scandalous reputations of the surrounding hotels. In his memoir *Surrender: 40 Songs, One Story*, Bono wrote about U2's first stay on Sunset. "That first time, in March 1981, we stayed in a properly rock n roll hotel called the Sunset Marquis," he wrote. "Out of the door, we could walk up the hill and around the corner to the Sunset Strip. Where for all its supposed worldliness, the neon—like us at twenty years old—felt naively drawn. I know the underbelly was there, but we hadn't the eyes to see it."[134] In addition to its minimal decadence, the Sunset Marquis was an inspired choice in accommodations. In the early 80s, the hotel was still subjectively accessible and unextravagant for those at the threshold of stardom.

When *The Hollywood Reporter* published a slick history of rock music's devotion to the Sunset Marquis in 2013, original U2 manager Paul McGuinness—then on the cusp of retirement—shared memories that fell far short of the ritzy reputation the hotel now enjoys. "It was inexpensive," McGuiness said. "You had a direct line to Turner's liquor store, though. So there was a sort of self-catering."[135] This was likely a reference to Gil Turner's Fine Wines and Spirits, which is still located at 9101 Sunset.

Meeting the Band in a Bygone Era – Fan Anecdotes

Throughout the 80s and 90s, many fans were able to meet the members of U2 the old fashioned way by loitering near the hotel's famous awning on Alta Loma Road—a fixture that declares the 1200 street address number in an elegant art deco typeface. The handful of Sunset Strip fan anecdotes featured in this book, starting with Ryan Carroll's story in the previous chapter and concluding with the two stories below, describe very different experiences that nonetheless share an important common thread: a lingering,

---

133 Greene, Andy. "20 Insanely Great U2 Songs Only Hardcore Fans Know." *Rolling Stone*, March 14, 2014.

134 Bono. 2022. *Surrender: 40 Songs, One Story*. Penguin Random House.

135 Baum, Gary, and Michael Walker. "Sunset Marquis: Secrets of Rock 'N' Roll's Wild Hotel." *The Hollywood Reporter*, February 8, 2013. https://www.hollywoodreporter.com/news/general-news/sunset-marquis-secrets-rock-n-419290/.

powerful nostalgia for the bygone era of meeting your favorite band outside their hotel.

Bono on Your Back

Simone Trimm was twenty-seven when she met Bono outside the Sunset Marquis on November 14, 1992, hours before the band would take ZooTV to Anaheim Stadium. She shared that for her autograph request, she turned around so he could sign the back of her bootlegged t-shirt. To this day, she still can't believe what he scribbled. "I kept asking people what he wrote," she shared, "because obviously I couldn't take it off! I couldn't believe he was writing something on my back." In Sharpie scroll, he had simply written, "Bono on your back."

Enter the Chateau Marmont

Seven months earlier, the band was in town for the first leg of the tour. It was April 1992, and Rhonda Sayers Wood would meet the band during their stay at the Sunset Marquis before one of the two nights that ZooTV would inhabit the Los Angeles Sports Arena. "I can't remember how I found out about the Sunset Marquis," she explained. "But I'm sure it was from an internet group." Internet, in

'92? "Yes," she replied with a laugh. "AOL, probably." It was the first in a series of face-to-face greetings that would go on for years—sometimes at the Marquis, and sometimes at another historic establishment one mile north: the legendary Chateau Marmont.

Sunset Marquis, 1992
Submitted by Rhonda Sayers Wood

The Chateau's notorious reputation has connections to every category of artist, from actors, to writers, to musicians. John Belushi met his tragic fate there, and Jim Morrison had lived in a poolside bungalow before moving to his final residence in France.

U2's exploits at the Chateau are hardly as infamous, but the band was known to begin staying there by the late 90s.

Bono Holds Your Baby

One such stay was in 1999, when Bono was in town for the Grammys and staying at the Chateau. Sayers-Wood recalled how he recognized her as he walked toward the small group of fans who had been gathering in a designated spot outside the hotel since the day prior. "There were four of us waiting," she told me. "He said that he didn't have time to talk to us, but if we came back tomorrow, he would make time." They did—and that time, Rhonda brought her infant son, Weston. "I had to take the baby with me," she said. "I remember Bono saying, 'Oh, you had a baby.'" His reply when she asked to hand her young one over for a photo was a kind "Sure"—but when she did, her son began to cry, and the rock star response did not disappoint. "Bono was cute and decided to suck his thumb," she recalled. Six years later, another encounter led to him signing the photo he took with the baby. He wrote, "Weston is now six. So is Bono."

This book only features three first person anecdotes about meeting U2 at the two hospitality beacons of the Sunset Strip, but many other fan stories can be found online. One was shared by the Sunset Marquis on its Instagram page on September 12, 2020: "If you stand right in this spot, you can softly here the music of @ u2 playing. Or so the legend goes. Anyone else have classic '1200' awning photos? #Repost Pete Segura on Facebook: 'I once met Bono. This was taken right after the "Where the Streets Have No Name" video shoot in downtown LA. That's my sister Susana Segura with the hat over his shoulder.'"[136]

Experiences like these would be difficult (if not impossible) to replicate now. Eventually, the Sunset Marquis added an underground parking structure so that notable guests could enter the property more privately. In addition, at least two U2 members (first Edge, then Bono)—due to acquiring their own respective Los Angeles real estate properties in the coming years—would become less likely to check into either of the two hotels,

---

136 "If you stand right in this spot, you can softly here the music of @u2 playing. Or so the legend goes."
www.instagram.com/SunsetMarquis/. September 12, 2020.

Home Away from Home

Although the band members no longer frequent the Sunset Marquis, some in their crew have continued to book their stays there when touring brings the U2 circus to Los Angeles.

One of them was tour manager Dennis Sheehan, who passed away in his hotel room the evening of May 26, 2015, hours after the band finished the first night of a nearly week-long residency at the Inglewood Forum on the *Innocence + Experience Tour* (often abbreviated as the *I+E* tour).

U2's longtime tour manager, Dennis Sheehan, was found dead Wednesday morning (May 27) in his hotel room in West Hollywood. He was 68.[137]

– The Hollywood Reporter, May 27, 2015

Sheehan's death at the Sunset Marquis made an indelible mark on the *I+E* tour. When the show went on at the Forum the following night, the band paid tribute to the man who had managed every U2 tour since 1982. Bono delivered this monologue to the crowd to dedicate the song "Iris," written about his late mother, to Sheehan:

"It takes a lot to put on a show like tonight—and last night, we lost a member of our family. Dennis Sheehan was his name. He was U2's tour manager for thirty-three years. He loved, as we all do, the city of Los Angeles, and he called the Sunset Marquis his "home away from home."[138]

– Bono, May 27, 2015

As the show concluded, Bono dedicated a second song to Sheehan—a fan favorite not previously considered for the setlist. "This next song will always be about Dennis Sheehan, and here's why," he said.

"We made a live album way back when...called *Under a Blood Red Sky*. We used to end the show with '40.' And whatever happened that night [at Red Rocks], nobody was singing the refrain.

---

137 Lynch, Joe. "U2'S Longtime Tour Manager Dennis Sheehan Found Dead." *The Hollywood Reporter*, May 27, 2015. https://www.hollywoodreporter.com/music/music-news/u2s-longtime-tour-manager-dennis-798317/.

138 "U2 at The Forum Pay Tribute to Dennis Sheehan." *The Hollywood Reporter*. May 27, 2015. Video, https://www.youtube.com/watch?v=h4HwuQsXinI&t=4s.

So we were backstage just trying to figure out what the hell was going on and trying to make it happen. We just heard this lone voice, this single voice, singing 'How long to sing this song'—a light voice, beautiful tremolo. And it was the voice of Dennis Sheehan, trying to get everyone to sing, which they did. So we dedicate this song—in fact, we dedicate the night—in fact, we dedicate our whole tour to the very vivid memory of Dennis Sheehan: St. Dennis of Dublin, as he's known around here."

It's About Surrender

Earlier in the show, "Bad"—a song Bono originally wrote for *The Unforgettable Fire* about childhood friend Andy Rowen's trauma and addiction—was introduced as an opportunity for audience members to embrace whatever personal meaning the lyrics held for them. As Edge's acclaimed modulated delay signaled the beginning of one of the most beloved anthems in the U2 catalog, Bono mused, "It's about surrender, it's an important word. This is about letting go, just anything you want to let go of, just let go of it tonight, anything, anything, anything that's going on."

"Bad" was not part of the planned set that night, as evidenced by its absence from the printed setlist.[139] Also included was a lyrical change made especially for the location, when "into the half-light and through the flame" became "into the half-light, California rain."

Although it was not explicitly stated, it stands to reason that these deviations took place because of the energy and emotions felt by the band in light of Sheehan's passing. He died doing what he had devoted decades of his life to: managing a U2 tour. Because of Sheehan's death at the Sunset Marquis, May 27, 2015 is remembered as one of the most structurally fluid nights of the *I+E* tour. A review in *Billboard* included this reflection:

To the question of whether Wednesday night's U2 show was demonstrably more emotional than usual in response to the death that morning of longtime tour manager Dennis Sheehan, you'd almost have to ask: How would you know, exactly? If the Stones long ago locked down

---

139 "U2 Innocence + Experience Tour Innocence + Experience Tour Leg 1: North America 2015-05-27: The Forum - Inglewood, California, USA." U2gigs.Com. https://www.u2gigs.com/show1919.html.

the phrase "world's greatest rock 'n' roll band," U2 is the world's most heart-on-sleeve rock 'n' roll band, at least in the heavyweight division ... Even a fresher intimation of mortality isn't going to totally transform the character of a U2 show: They're already most of the way there.

But they got a little further at Wednesday's Forum show in Los Angeles ... Sheehan's death wasn't dwelled upon at length, but did become the focus of two monologues, one funny, one more touching. So if on his behalf U2 could revive something that seemingly moribund and re-embrace all the meaning it ever once had and still could have, yes, they loved the guy.[140]

The death of Dennis Sheehan, U2's tour manager of three decades, reinforced the band's ties to Los Angeles in a way no one could have predicted—and it happened at the Sunset Marquis, the band's first LA "home."

Top left by Brook W. Flagg

Middle left by Pete Segura

Bottom left by Brook W. Flagg

Top right, Wikimedia Commons

Middle right courtesy of Rhonda Sayers Wood

Bottom right, Wikimedia Commons

140 Willman, Chris. "U2 Delivers Life-Affirming Show Following Tour Manager's Unexpected Death." *Billboard*, May 28, 2015. https://www.billboard.com/music/music-news/u2-innocence-experience-tour-forum-dennis-sheehan-6582845/.

the hotels today

*By Pete Segura
(1987)*

*Rhonda & Weston
w/Bono (1999)*

*Wendy, Novelle
Brook, Noemi
(2022)*

*the Chateau
at night*

Book Soup, Source of Design Inspiration for *The Joshua Tree*

It's not the only bookstore on the Sunset Strip, but it *is* the only one to rightly proclaim itself "Bookseller to the Great and Infamous." Since 1975, Book Soup has built its reputation by leaning into its origin story (it was founded by two UCLA grad students with just $50,000, at a location that is now multi-million dollar prime real estate); holding live author readings on an almost daily basis; and, being willing participants in various celebrity author-related publicity stunts.

Case in point: in 1988, when a fatwa was issued condemning *The Satanic Verses* by Salman Rushdie (who became a friend of U2 as a result), Book Soup co-owner Glenn Goldman wrote a ransom note to the *LA Times* declaring that freedom of speech was being held hostage.

Another 1980s Book Soup connection to U2 came courtesy of the band's primary designer Stephen Averill, who stated on the *U2-Y* podcast that the shop was where he found inspiration for *The Joshua Tree* imagery. "There was a place called Book Soup … full of fascinating books on design and Americana and all sorts of things. I could have bought a trunk full of reference points."[141]

The connection doesn't end there; three decades later, the Sunset Strip's most prominent bookstore would become a U2 microcosm one more time.

Book Soup, Site of *Surrender* Fan Shenanigans

More than thirty years after Stephen Averill found inspiration for the aesthetics of *The Joshua Tree* tour at Book Soup, the retailer would play a supporting role in a U2-adjacent project.

Bono's 2022 memoir *Surrender: 40 Songs, One Story* was distributed by independent bookstores around the world; some of them hosted his brief, unpublicized appearances, while others were simply drop-off points or hubs for distribution. In many major cities, fans flocked to whatever local bookseller they hoped would be the chosen distributor, especially on the day of Bono's scheduled *Stories of Surrender* book tour performance in each city.

---

141 Averill, Stephen. "Chapter 6 - The Joshua Tree." U2-Y Podcast. May 29, 2023.

On the November weekend of his performance at the Orpheum Theater in Los Angeles, hopeful fans stationed themselves outside two specific book shops: The Last Bookstore at 453 Spring Street, and Book Soup at 8818 Sunset. Although a personal Bono appearance ultimately did not happen at either spot, one of the two stores was indeed the chosen vendor to supply the books: Book Soup, the Sunset Strip store that had been known to the U2 camp for decades.

On November 14, roughly a dozen of the more than one hundred fans who were disappointed that Bono had not shown up the previous day at The Last Bookstore gathered in and around Book Soup for one last attempt at a run-in. Because the American leg of his *Stories of Surrender* tour ended in LA and the European leg would commence in London just three days later, the fans were hopeful that Bono might breeze through the store on his way out of town to sign books en route to his flight. Frustrated Book Soup employees informed them that no, Bono *had not* been there and *would not* be there.

What those fans saw instead were palettes of *Surrender* books being delivered to the store, sans the author—and yet, what they experienced was still peak Sunset Strip culture (as much as midlife mischief and mayhem could be).

After hours of buying magazines and other merchandise to avoid getting evicted from the store and hiding among the ceiling-high shelves of stock, only three fans—two from California, one from Australia—remained in the store as their peers, one by one, gave up and went home. The three women giggled as they eavesdropped on a burly, bearded motorcyclist wearing a *The Joshua Tree 2017* tour jacket who entered the store sometime after 5 p.m. to inquire about Bono's possible arrival. A frustrated store employee humored him for all of twenty seconds as he pressed her for information: *had* Bono been there, *would* Bono be there? After all, he told her, "I thought he might be driving around with Sean Penn and decide to stop in to sign a few books."

For the three women hiding among the shelves (one of whom was this book's author), the well-meaning man's antiquated, late-80s fantasy that the frontman for U2 would still operate this way was sweet, charming, and affirming of their own choice to hang around the store until sundown approached. The employee, however, was not amused.

"No," she said flatly. She had rightly had her fill of rabid, middle-aged U2 fans for one day. As the man left, the three hiding fans giggled with reckless abandon. It was their queue—well, *our* queue—to give up and go home. But it sure was fun while it lasted.

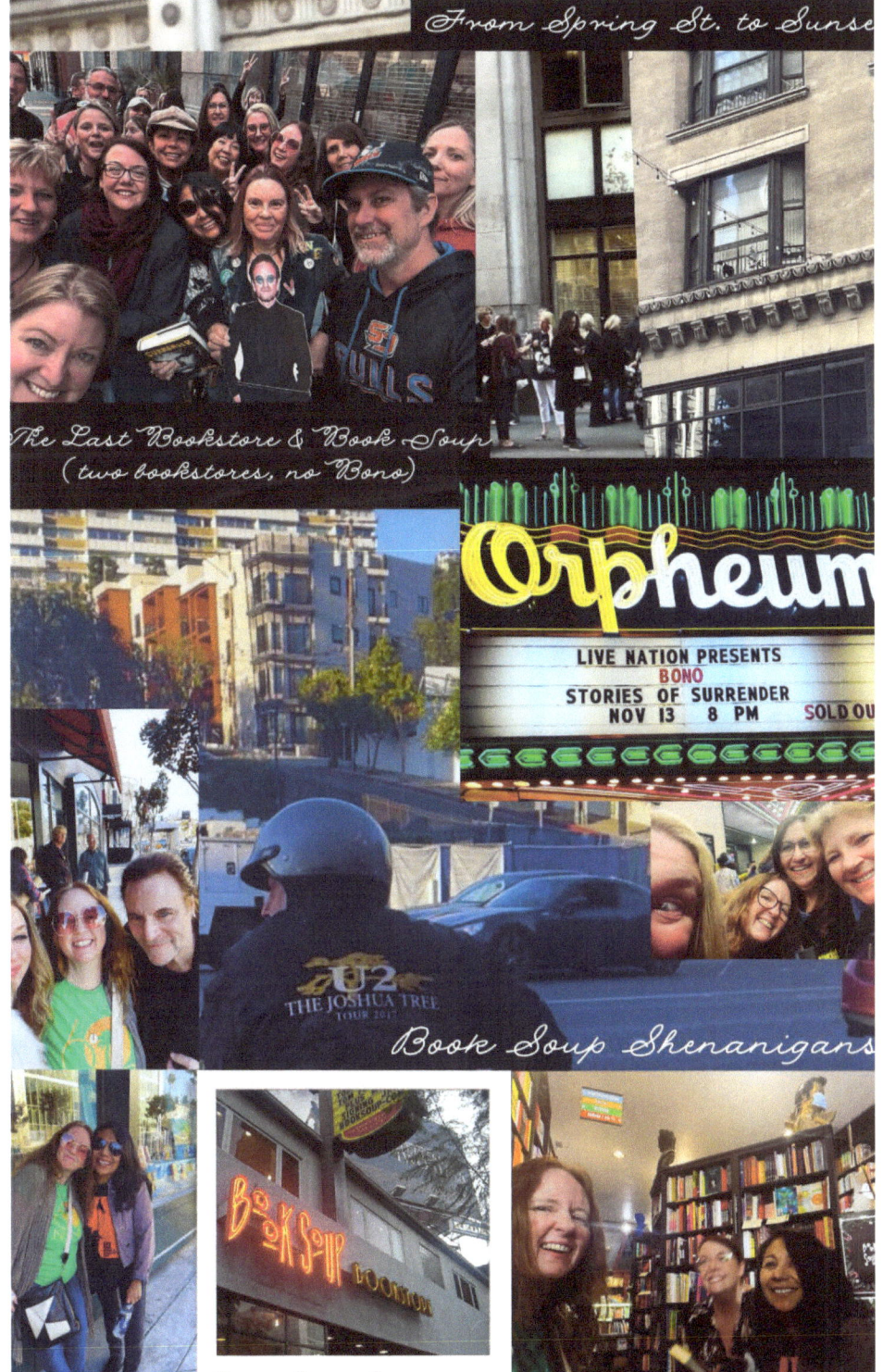

From Spring St. to Sunse[t]

The Last Bookstore & Book Soup
(two bookstores, no Bono)

Orpheum

LIVE NATION PRESENTS
BONO
STORIES OF SURRENDER
NOV 13   8 PM   SOLD OU[T]

U2
THE JOSHUA TREE
TOUR 2017

Book Soup Shenanigans

BOOK SOUP BOOKSHOP

Book Soup Storefront

The Roxy Theatre

Location: 9009 Sunset Blvd., West Hollywood

Significance: Only show on the Sunset Strip; only club show of I+E tour; contest winner admittance only

Date in U2 history: May 28, 2015

Still in operation/visitable? Yes

"We had some fun and frolics at the Roxy the night before last. It was interesting."[142]

– Bono, live at the Forum, May 30, 2015

Throughout 2015, the emphasis on U2's roots and connection to early punk rock ensured that the band's club show days would be referenced frequently during the *Innocence + Experience* tour. However, the only site of an actual U2 club show on the *I+E* tour was in West Hollywood, when the band paused its five-night residency at the Forum in Inglewood to play an exclusive show at the Sunset Strip's historic Roxy Theatre. The show was arranged as a consolation for U2 canceling what would have been their first appearance at KROQ's annual holiday charity festival, *Almost Acoustic Christmas*, when the band was forced to back out after Bono's bicycling injuries in November 2014.[143]

Lucky Callers & Luminaries

Unfortunately for fans who purchased tickets for the KROQ event solely based on U2's appearance, that investment would not guarantee entrance to the Roxy; admittance to the club show was available exclusively to contest winners, with the exception of luminaries such as Jack Nicholson, Tom Morello, Courtney Love,

---

142 "Iris by U2 at the Forum, May 30, 2015." Lauren Huynh. May 31, 2015. Video, https://www.youtube.com/watch?v=GrLiAyBJhuc&list=RDGrLiAyBJhuc&start_radio=1.

143 Appleford, Steve. "U2 Play Old Hits, Share Stories at Thrilling 500-Capacity Roxy Gig." *Rolling Stone*, May 29, 2015.

and Aaron Paul, all of whom received invitations.[144] By the KROQ events department's own admission at the time, the strong celebrity presence took up so much space that the station was prevented from accommodating ticket requests from U2 fan-based media (at the time, this book's author attempted to obtain an admission pass as a writer for the fansite U2 Zoo Station Radio).

In the week leading up to the show, KROQ organizers leveraged the classic "lucky caller" contest model of FM radio's prime by prompting listeners to call into their contest line at the top of every hour to try for tickets. Thousands of fans called, but only a few hundred won. During what was already shaping up to be a whirlwind week for Southern California fans, the rare opportunity to attend an intimate club show was a bittersweet reality for those who missed out. For those who did make it in, the reality was sublime. "I was at work when I won," Courtney Lavender shared, "and the next winner an hour later was my roommate. I was stoked my time had finally come. It was so surreal!"

In a news update titled "A Night at the Roxy," the official band website U2.com reported on the event. (As an aside, this entry referenced the Reseda Country Club without mentioning it by name):

After two nights of a five-night stand at the Forum, the band went back in time last night, returning to their club roots to play the 500-capacity Roxy, their first show in such an intimate LA area venue in decades. If the U2ie Tour has been reinventing the arena show as an intimate tour de force, this scrappy, charged club gig for a few hundred lucky KROQ contest winners packed a stadium's worth of energy—from crowd and band alike—into a club the size of the first LA venue the band ever played.[145]

– "A Night at the Roxy," U2.com

Stuck in a Moment

May 26–31 began as a celebratory week of U2 descending upon Los Angeles—but almost immediately, the band was blindsided by the sudden death of tour manager Dennis Sheehan in his Sunset

---

144 Ibid.

145 "A Night at the Roxy." U2.Com. May 29, 2015. https://www.u2.com/news/title/a-night-at-the-roxy/.

Marquis hotel room. Although Bono paid tribute to Sheehan during night two at the Forum, he did so again at the Roxy.

After a fitting rendition of "Stuck in a Moment You Can't Get Out Of," which had not yet been played on the *I+E* tour until that night, Bono told the crowd:

"You know, if your life's spent trying to (focus on) what you put on your CV, and then that suddenly doesn't mean anything when they're putting you in the ground. And the eulogy of who you are just becomes everything. Not what you did, but who you are. And this Dennis Sheehan, if you could sense the love and best wishes we've had in the last twenty-four hours from all over the world ... everyone was touched by him. Just a gentleman. He actually had the dignity that our music aspires to. He had that dignity. The dignity that we all aspire to, he had it."[146]

– Bono, live at the Roxy, May 28, 2015

Five *Boy*-Era Songs

To mark the band's one-night return to the club scene, an unusually high volume of *Boy*-era songs was played—five in total.

1. "The Ocean"

For the first time since June 8, 1981, a U2 show opened with *Boy*'s seventh track "The Ocean"—a song that had not been played in ten years since the *Vertigo* tour.[147] At the conclusion of the song, Bono recited the 1934 poem "Do Not Stand at My Grave and Weep" by Clare Harner—an appropriate inclusion for a time when themes of death and grief were at the forefront for U2. Given the inclusion of this poem, it seems plausible that "The Ocean" returning to the set almost nightly three years later on the *Experience + Innocence* tour as an introduction to "Iris" (a song about death and grief) was predicated by its use as the opening song at the Roxy, where it set the tone for a night of grieving and healing.

---

146 "U2 West Hollywood Roxy Theatre California." Lorna Cairns. May 28, 2015.
    Video, https://www.youtube.com/watch?v=F29CES6_4mA.

147 "U2 Boy Tour Boy 5th Leg: European Summer Shows 1981-06-08: Sportpark - Geleen, Netherlands."
    U2gigs.Com. https://www.u2gigs.com/show474.html.

2. "11 O'Clock Tick Tock"

The next surprise came with the first notes of "11 O'Clock Tick Tock," the first performance of the song since August 21, 2001.[148] While not included on *Boy* due to the timing of its recording in April 1980 and the band's poor experience with producer Martin Hannett, the song was only released as a single. However, because it was U2's first release with Island Records, released the same year as *Boy*, and played more than 120 times on the *Boy* tour, "11 O'Clock Tick Tock" is generally regarded as a product of the band's *Boy* era. In the 2015 Roxy performance, Bono changed one of the song's most recognizable lyrics ("We thought that we had the answers") to "*You* thought that we had the answers."[149] Perhaps this was an acknowledgment of the tough public relations year that had transpired for U2—and by extension, their fans—kicked off by the controversy surrounding the innovative move to release *Songs of Innocence* for free to Apple users.

3. "I Will Follow"

Continuing the Roxy set's *Boy*-era beginning was "I Will Follow," the only song to be played on every tour in U2 history (with the exception of the *U2:UV* Las Vegas residency). After the second verse, Bono briefly entered the first rows of the crowd, allowing them to hold him up as he sang the "Your eyes" bridge of the song. It should be noted that on many occasions throughout the *I+E* tour and the two tours that followed it, Bono used this section of "I Will Follow" to repeat a message of thanks to KROQ for being one of the first American radio stations to play the song on their air. The 2015 Roxy performance was an exception, as his words of gratitude for KROQ would come later in the show after a snippet of the Ramones' "I Remember You" ended "Beautiful Day"—and then, a second time during his comments before "California (There is No End to Love),"

---

148 "11 O'Clock Tick Tock." U2gigs.com. https://www.u2gigs.com/11_OClock_Tick_Tock-s52.html.

149 "U2 West Hollywood Roxy Theatre California." Lorna Cairns. May 28, 2015.
   Video, https://www.youtube.com/watch?v=F29CES6_4mA.

the final song of the show. "We had arrived on our very first tour; KROQ were playing 'I Will Follow' on the radio all the time," he said.[150]

4. "The Electric Co."

When "The Electric Co." was played for the first time in eighteen years, it was for another audience of radio callers: two nights before the first show of the Vertigo tour, for 600 contest winners at the Los Angeles Sports Arena. It would be played seventy-six times on that tour, giving fans of the punk-powered opening lyric "Boy, stupid boy" their fill throughout 2005–06. But the song went away for the next nine years, absent from all seven legs of the *U2 360°* tour.[151] When it made a return to the set, it would be in San Jose, at the fourth show of the *I+E* tour; it would also be played the first night at the Forum. Seemingly, neither of those instances dulled fans' appetite for the song at the Roxy. When viewing the show on YouTube, one might sense U2's intention to pay tribute to the utmost LA club band, The Doors, as the bridge of this song begins around 14:00.

5. "Out of Control"

For those who relish live performances of *Boy* material, enthusiasm for "The Electric Co." is rarely superseded—but fanaticism for U2's first single, released in September 1979, may be the exception. Although "Out of Control" has never left the live U2 set for as long as "The Electric Co." and both songs were played regularly throughout the *I+E* tour (thirty times and thirty-three times, respectively), it was a rarity for both songs to be played on the same night. The Roxy performance was that rarity.

This Sacramental Friendship

Amid the band's varying public reputations that have formed over the decades, the most devoted fans understand that at the heart of U2 is the friendship of four boys who formed a band—and that, as those boys grew into men over five decades, their friendship

---

150 Ibid.

151 "The Electric Co." U2gigs.com. https://www.u2gigs.com/The_Electric_Co_-s189.html.

evolved into a brotherhood. It was likely in this spirit that Bono improvised these thoughts from the Roxy stage:

"Alright, this sacramental music, this sacramental friendship that is at the heart of this band, yeah, music and friendship, and the idea that even friendship … friendship is higher than love."[152]

Tying those thoughts into the loss of Dennis Sheehan, he elaborated:

"We've lost a friend, and he's our workmate, but friendship … you know, you fight with your friends, you love your friends, you go out with your friends, you work with your friends … it's kind of a dysfunctional family, the U2 situation, but actually quite functional in other ways, as we do look after each other."[153]

– Bono, live at the Roxy, May 28, 2015

If one strength emerged out of the U2 camp during the *I+E* tour, it was the persistent referencing of the band's history. That strength was on full display the week of the band's Los Angeles mini-residency. Once again likening their club show revival at the Roxy in 2015 to their first California show at Reseda Country Club in 1981, U2.com reported:

Like that show, way back in 1981, the setlist at The Roxy shared five songs with the U.S. Boy Tour setlist. The show opened with "The Ocean" as the band did so often back in those days, likewise careening into a furious 11 O'Clock Tick Tock reappearing for the first time since 2001.[154]

– "A Night at the Roxy," U2.com

Indeed, it was the first time "11 O'Clock Tick Tock" had been played since August 21, 2001, when it was played at Earl's Court Arena in London on the second leg of the *Elevation* tour. Even so, at least one front-row fan in the club that night shouted a request for it to be played a second time. Bono addressed the request: "We used to play '11 O'Clock Tick Tock' and 'I Will Follow' twice," he said. "We won't

---

152 "U2 West Hollywood Roxy Theatre California." Lorna Cairns. May 28, 2015.
   Video, https://www.youtube.com/watch?v=F29CES6_4mA.

153 Ibid.

154 "A Night at the Roxy." U2.Com. May 29, 2015. https://www.u2.com/news/title/a-night-at-the-roxy/.

be doing that this evening. Thank you for your suggestion. Always welcome. Zootopians never fail," he concluded, acknowledging the name of the official fan community platform on U2.com.[155]

Zuma Mystery Solved

As explained in Section V, Bono solved the Zuma Beach mystery of the song "California" on this night at the Roxy. When viewing the show on YouTube, fans can revisit his comments on the band discovering Zuma in a quest to find the home of Brian Wilson."[156]

In a recap of the Roxy show, Steve Appleford wrote for *Rolling Stone*:

At night's end, he spoke of U2's first trip to Los Angeles and a visit to Zuma Beach in search of Brian Wilson's house. He noted there was a Beach Boys album at U2's first rehearsal in 1976. "We heard he had a piano in a sand pit and we just thought this man had the music of the spheres," Bono said as the band eased into Songs of Innocence's celebratory "California (There Is No End to Love)." They added a bit of the Beach Boys' "God Only Knows" and closed a short but potent set with a forceful, mystical sound of their own.[157]

Like the first American club shows on the *Boy* tour more than three decades earlier—including their first Los Angeles performance at Reseda Country Club—U2's night at the Roxy was all at once gritty, gleaming, and glorious.

Photo courtesy of Courtney Lavender

155 "U2 West Hollywood Roxy Theatre California." Lorna Cairns. May 28, 2015.
      Video, https://www.youtube.com/watch?v=F29CES6_4mA.

156 Ibid.

157 Appleford, Steve. "U2 Play Old Hits, Share Stories at Thrilling 500-Capacity Roxy Gig."
      Rolling Stone, May 29, 2015.

Roxy photos by Courtney Lavender
Additional elements/collage by Brook W. Flagg

Canter's Deli

Location: 419 North Fairfax Avenue, Los Angeles
Significance: Visit from Bono during *I+E* tour LA shows + on-stage endorsement
Date in U2 history: May 28, 2015
Still in operation/visitable? Yes, with patronage

"I went to Canter's the night before last. There's a woman who's there ... She was there in the 80s; I think she was there in the 60s. She was beautiful, and she knew what I wanted to order."[158]

– Bono, live at the Forum, May 30, 2015

The roughly ten-day stretch in which U2 inhabited Los Angeles for a five-night run at the Forum and a rare club show at the Roxy in the final week of May/first week of June 2015 was marked by at least one unscheduled appearance of the band's frontman. Bono, his childhood friend Derek Rowen (better known as the Irish artist Guggi), and a third unnamed companion arrived at the famed Canter's Deli sometime after midnight on May 28 for a late-night meal—a meal that made national news due to his generous tip and on-stage subsequent endorsement.

Canter's Deli History

Located in the historically Jewish community known as the Fairfax District, Canter's Deli is a Jewish-style delicatessen that opened in 1931 and first occupied its permanent spot at 419 North Fairfax Avenue in 1948. More restaurant than deli due to its massive multi-room layout, Canter's is known for its extensive menu of award-winning breakfasts, dinners, and traditional deli favorites including pastrami, corned beef, and flavored cream cheeses to spread over house-made bagels. Its mostly 24-hour operation (with exception to the Jewish holidays of Rosh Hashanah and Yom Kippur) makes Canter's a favorite for locals and tourists seeking a quality all-night dining option in LA.

---

158 "Iris by U2 at the Forum, May 30, 2015." Lauren Huynh. May 31, 2015.
    Video, https://www.youtube.com/watch?v=GrLiAyBJhuc&list=RDGrLiAyBJhuc&start_radio=1.

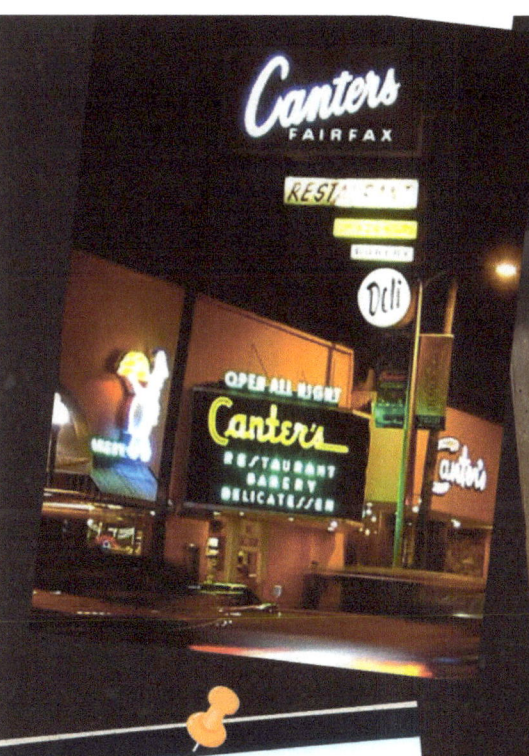

Billboard

U2's Bono Noshes at Canters Deli, Leaves $150 Tip

What's for dinner? Corned beef reuben, fries and rugelach on the house.

Leave it to Bono to make a Los Angeles waitress' night.

The U2 frontman went for a late-night meal at L.A. landmark Canters Deli on Saturday night where he was waited on by a 50-year veteran of the restaurant.

According to a source, the rocker asked his server to pick out his meal, which she did, bringing out a veritable mish-mash of classic Jewish deli fare including a corned beef reuben, french fries and onion rings. For dessert: chocolate chip rugelach on the house.

Bono left a $150 tip for the waitress, on a bill that totaled less than $20.

Canters later got a shout-out on the U2 website, which noted, "U2's love for L.A. was proclaimed - all of L.A. - downtown, the valleys, the canyons, and its feeling of 'what might be.'"

"I went to Canter's the night before last. There's a woman who's there...

...She was there in the 80s; I think she was there in the 60s. She was beautiful, and she knew what I wanted to order."

— Bono | May 30, 2015

Canter's Connection to Music

Celebrities from all corners of show business, including musicians, have frequented Canter's over the years to dine alongside everyday patrons. Guns N' Roses still has a dedicated table adorned with an early photo due to the band's friendship with co-owner Marc Canter, who wrote a book on them called *Reckless Road: Guns N' Roses and The Making of Appetite for Destruction*.[159] Another example is Jakob Dylan, Bob Dylan's son and frontman of The Wallflowers; he first met the future members of his band in the Kibitz Room, Canter's bar space marketed as "the kookiest dive bar ever hidden inside a famous LA deli."[160] The Kibitz Room is known for nightly live music performances; however, U2 fans who wish to replicate Bono's 2015 visit should know that his party sat in Canter's primary dining area.

Bono's Corned Beef Reuben

This *Billboard* report documenting the visit is framed and mounted near Canter's bakery counter:

U2's Bono Noshes at Canter's Deli, Leaves $150 Tip

Leave it to Bono to make a Los Angeles waitress' night. The U2 frontman went for a late-night meal at L.A. landmark Canter's Deli on Saturday night where he was waited on by a 50-year veteran of the restaurant. According to a source, the rocker asked his server to pick out his meal, which she did, bringing out a veritable mish-mash of classic Jewish deli fare including a corned beef reuben, french fries and onion rings. For dessert: chocolate chip rugelach on the house.

Bono left a $150 tip for the waitress, on a bill that totaled less that $20.

Canters later got a shout-out on the U2 website, which noted, "U2's love for L.A. was proclaimed–all of LA–downtown, the valleys, the canyons, and its feeling of 'what might be.'"

U2 wraps a five-night, standing-room-only run at The Forum on Wednesday, June 3.[161]

159 Canter, Marc. 2008. *Reckless Road: Guns N' Roses and the Making of Appetite for Destruction.* Music Sales America.

160 Wild, David . "Q&A: Jakob Dylan." *Rolling Stone*, January 22, 1998. https://www.rollingstone.com/music/music-news/qa-jakob-dylan-186252/.

161 Brandle, Lars. "U2'S Bono Noshes at Canters Deli, Leaves $150 Tip." Billboard, June 1, 2015. https://www.billboard.com/music/music-news/u2s-bono-noshes-at-canters-deli-in-la-leaves-150-tip-6583059/.

Grammy Museum Sidewalk at LA Live

> **Location:** 800 W. Olympic Blvd., Los Angeles
>
> **Significance:** Plaques commemorating a portion of U2's Grammy wins
>
> **Still in operation/visitable?** Yes

"We shall continue to abuse our position and fuck up the mainstream."[162]
— Bono, live at *The Grammy Awards*, March 1, 1994

A handful of U2's twenty-two Grammy Awards are commemorated on bronze disc plaques outside the Grammy Museum in the LA Live district. The plaques, which were embedded into the sidewalk when the museum opened in December 2008, honor Grammy winners dating back to 1959.

U2 appears on two plaques, which can be found on the east side of the building facing Figueroa Street. They signify a small portion of the band's overall Grammy wins—namely for *All That You Can't Leave Behind* in 2002 and *How to Dismantle an Atomic Bomb* in 2006, the band's most recent releases to win Grammys at the time of the museum's opening. U2 shares space on their plaques with other artists, including Alicia Keys, Green Day, and John Legend.

The sidewalk plaques are in a public space that can be easily visited by fans, free of charge, any time of year. There is no permanent U2 exhibit inside the museum.

Grammy Museum
sidewalk plaques

GRAMMY MUSEUM

LBUM OF THE YEAR
U2
HOW TO DISMANTLE AN
ATOMIC BOMB

SONG OF THE YEAR
SOMETIMES YOU CAN'T
MAKE IT ON YOUR OWN
Bono, Adam Clayton, The Edge
& Larry Mullen Jr. Songwriters
February 8, 2006

RECORD OF THE
U2
WALK ON

4th GRAMMY AWARD

October 2022

A Celebration: The Original U2 LA Fan Club

Location: 1110 N. Hudson Avenue, Los Angeles

Significance: Historically largest in-person U2 fan club in the U.S.

Dates in U2 history: March 2, 1985–September 14, 1988

Still in operation? No

Building still standing? Yes

A CELEBRATION

AN ORGANIZATION TOUCHED BY THE MUSIC OF U2

"A CELEBRATION is...
  * *A non-profit, philanthropic group interested in supporting the bands who stand for a cause. New idealism and non-partisan peace.*
  * *U2 fans gathering to celebrate the music of U2."*

  – From club mission statement, 1987

Before there were online fan communities, there were live fan clubs that held in-person meetings with agendas and activities. At the height of U2's global 1980s popularity, Los Angeles was—for a time—home to the largest live U2 fan club in America, and possibly the world.

First Meeting: Pan Pacific Park

The group called itself A Celebration; it was named by co-founders Corey Lesh, Ellen McCurdy, and Julie Borchard after the 1982 standalone single designed to fill the gap between the *October* and *War* albums. The first meeting was held at Pan Pacific Park in Hollywood on March 2, 1985, the first day of U2's three-night run at the LA Sports Arena on *The Unforgettable Fire* tour. Eventually, meetings moved to the Lhasa Club, a venue that the *Los Angeles Times* said was "located on a small, dark side street off Santa Monica Boulevard in Hollywood" (specifically, it was on the north end of Hudson Avenue).[163]

A "Mixed Bag" at the Lhasa

For just under six years until the doors closed in December 1987, the Lhasa showcased everything from cabaret acts and comedians to poets and other performance artists, in addition to musical acts that included Fatih No More and a young Chris Isaak.[164] But on the first Sunday of each month, A Celebration held its meetings of U2 fans ranging in age from their teens through 40s. When Steve Hochman showed up to do a profile for the *LA Times*, he estimated about 250 people in attendance, "representing the whole range of U2 fandom."[165]

"It is, undeniably, a mixed bag," Hochman wrote. "At one table, four youngsters sit and work on coloring books while their mother talks of her concern about the 'satanic' message communicated in most rock music. Nearby is a group of guys in their twenties, hard at work on a case of beer. Back in the corner of the room is a man sporting long hair, a tie-dyed shirt and—among a lot of Beatles buttons—a heart-shaped pin that reads LOVE-IN 87. That the music of U2 could draw these people into the same social setting along with the young, fresh-faced folks who make up the bulk of the crowd would be enough to support claims that U2's appeal is a singular phenomenon."[166]

One of the most frequent club attendees was Bill See, now co-host of the *Into the Heart of U2 Podcast*. He shared that from time to time, A Celebration meetings featured live performances from local bands—one of them being his. "[Lesh] had my band, Divine Weeks, play there once right before our first tour," See said. "I'll never forget he gave us a few bucks because we were so broke."

---

163 Cromelin, Richard. "POP WEEKEND : Doors Close, But L.A. Hasn't Seen the Last of Lhasa Club." *Los Angeles Times*, December 21, 1987.

164 Unknown. "LHASA CLUB." Punks on Acid. September 12, 2016. https://punks-on-acid.blogspot.com/2016/09/lhasa-club.html.

165 Hochman, Steve. "The Scene at the Coliseum: The Fans, The Media and The Music." *Los Angeles Times*, November 19, 1987.

166 Ibid.

Supporting U2-Aligned Causes

Rather than charging dues or an admission fee, A Celebration asked for a five-dollar donation per meeting. The proceeds were donated to two of the most high-visibility nonprofits of the time, Amnesty International and World Vision. When the club was founded, U2's support of Amnesty International was becoming well-known; in June 1986, the band played six shows for the *Conspiracy of Hope* tour benefiting the organization.

For A Celebration's final "last hurrah party" in September 1988, the seven-dollar cover charge would go to a timely cause of the late '80s: the AIDS Hospice Foundation.

An Acknowledgement from U2

Propaganda, the official fanzine from the band's "U2 World Service," published a splashy story on A Celebration in Volume 1, Issue 4. It included directions on how to reach the Lhasa for those who may wish to visit when in LA. In the same article, Bono supplied a remark that the club was "one thing this year [that] has made me feel better."[167]

"That was a huge thrill for us," Lesh said. "Made us feel like we were doing the right thing."

A CELEBRATION'S Julie Borchard (Right) presents Amnesty International's, Nadine Cohen a $100 check on Amnesty's 25th Anniversary of stopping the torture of international prisoners.

From *Propaganda U2 World Service Magazine*, Volume 1, Issue 4

The author thanks Corey Lesh for sharing the original promotional materials and press coverage for A Celebration, in addition to his reflections on the club's three-year run. "I have so many happy memories from those days," he said.

A Celebration literature courtesy of Corey Lesh

A Celebration press coverage courtesy of Corey Lesh

Club meeting performance photo courtesy of Bill See

A **U2**

"CELEBRATION"

A GATHERING EXTENDED TO ALL
WHO HAVE BEEN TOUCHED BY
THE MUSIC OF U2...

SATURDAY
MARCH 2nd • 2 PM

PAN PACIFIC
▲ **PARK** ▲
HOLLYWOOD

DIRECTIONS

1. HOLLYWOOD FREEWAY TO MELROSE
2. WEST ON MELROSE TO GARDNER = 3 mi.
3. SOUTH ON GARDNER TO 3rd = 1 mi.
4. ➡ CORNER GARDNER & 3rd !

Rejoice!

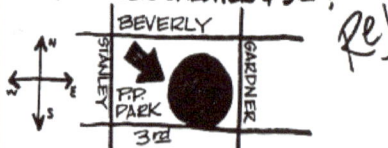

▲ CANNED AND BOXED
FOOD WILL BE COLLECTED
AT EACH U2 CONCERT DATE TO
FEED LA'S HUNGRY...
IN THE SPIRIT OF U2,
PLEASE HELP!

▲ BRING COLLECTABLES FOR
TRADING

▲ CARAVAN TO CONCERT

▲ QUESTIONS?
FOR MORE INFO CALL:

COREY (818) 448-9015
● ELLEN (213) 209-2970

OUR 6 MONTH
ANNIVERSARY!

A CELEBRATION
THE CLUB

FEATURING

◁ RARE VIDEOS AND MUSIC FROM U2, ALARM
AND OTHERS, INCLUDING THE FIRST U.S.
SCREENING OF THE U2 DOCUMENTARY --
"WIDE AWAKE IN AMERICA"

◁ LIVE ACOUSTIC SET --"CLOCKWORK"

◁ BRING CANNED AND BOXED FOOD FOR L.A.'s HOMELESS

SUNDAY
OCTOBER 5, 7-11
NO AGE LIMIT, ADMISSION $3.50

ALL PROCEEDS TO BENEFIT AMNESTY INTERNATIONAL

LHASA CLUB
1110 N. HUDSON AVE
HOLLYWOOD

HOLLYWOOD
FREEWAY
101

HIGHLAND
HUDSON
CAHUENGA

SANTA MONICA BLVD

A CELEBRATION · GROUP PHOTO · March 2, 1985

FRIDAY, APRIL 17, 1987

You, too, can be part of 'Celebration'

by CRAIG ROSEN
Daily News Staff Writer

Guests sign a flag that was given to Edge during U2's three night stop over in L.A.

ans Ellen McCurdy, Corey Lesh and Julie Borchard, from at Coliseum: Has cynicism replaced awesome and –

The Auld Dubliner Pub - Long Beach

Location: 71 S. Pine Avenue, Long Beach, CA 90802

Significance: Bono patronage with photos and signed Guinness certificate above bar

Date in U2 history: February 26, 2013

Still in operation/visitable? Yes, with patronage

"I thought, forget the rock opera, forget the bombast, the only thing I would be singing today is the facts. For I have truly embraced my inner nerd. So, exit the rock star. Enter the evidence activist. The 'factivist.'"[168]
                                                                    – Bono, live at TED2013

The Long Beach Convention Center was the site of the annual conference for the TED organization at the height of the TED Talk craze in 2013. TED2013, held from February 25 through March 1, was billed as "a week of ideas, connections, and fresh TED Talks"—one of which was delivered by Bono on February 26, the second day of the conference.

Bono's TED Talk, titled "The good news on poverty (Yes, there's good news)," addressed the progress made in fighting global poverty since he began working for the cause over a decade earlier. He encouraged continued efforts, emphasized the power of people working together, and projected hope for the coming decades, particularly due to the aid of technology and social media.

And then, he and his small entourage casually headed to the pub across the street.

That pub was the Auld Dubliner, founded by Long Beach native Eric Johnson and Irish-born David Copley. It's an authentic, contemporary Irish pub where both traditional main dishes and Americanized pub fare are on the menu. The atmosphere is a delight any time of day, as are the food and drink.

As of 2024, several servers who engaged with Bono during his visit were still on the job and happy to regale the account: where he sat, what he ate, and who among them was the first to suggest he pour himself a pint at the Guinness tap. Evidence of the visit has remained visible over the years, including a framed photo display behind the bar where he poured said pint. A "Great Guinness Award" certificate, signed by Bono during the visit with the numeral 13 handwritten under his name to commemorate the year, is also on display.

One day in 2013, Bono was in Long Beach just long enough to make the Auld Dubliner pub a site of significance for U2 fans to enjoy. If you go, tell them why you're there—and if you're lucky, they might let you stand at the Guinness tap.

Top left, photographer unknown

Collage and remaining photos by Brook W. Flagg

2013

2021

2024

n the wall

At the tap

Bono's table

SECTION V

Sites of Historical Significance in Los Angeles

KROQ PRESENTS

Sites of Historical Significance in LA

These sites are historic Los Angeles institutions, all of which are still in operation, that earn an honorable mention in U2 history.

The Hollywood Palladium

Built on the site of the original Paramount lot, the Palladium opened on Halloween night 1940 with Tommy Dorsey and his orchestra performing with featured vocalists, one of whom was Frank Sinatra.[169] Decades later, the Palladium would host REM ('84), the Smiths ('85), and Jane's Addiction ('90)—but U2 was there before any of them, stopping in for the second leg of the *October* tour on November 28, 1981.[170]

Even the Ramones—who have long been venerated by U2 and credited by Bono for awakening his calling as a performer—did not play the Palladium for the first time until three years *after* U2 in '84, co-headlining with Black Flag for a show remembered for its heavy police presence (an iconic photo of riot gear police marching into the venue directly under the marquee featuring the names of the two bands is preserved on the cover of Henry Rollins' 1994 tour diary memoir *Get in the Van*).[171] The Ramones would return to the Palladium several times over the next decade, including on their farewell *Adios Amigos* tour (an unforgettable first concert together for this book's author and her then-boyfriend/now-husband on August 29, 1995).

As for U2's Palladium stop in 1981, Terry Atkinson's *LA Times* review described a "powerful 80-minute set, an even more impressive performance than the group's local debut last March at the Country Club." The review continued, "After about an hour, many in the front ranks—from which about a dozen fans had previously leaped on stage to briefly dance alongside singer Bono Hewson—were standing on the stage lip. Some affectionately grappled for Hewson every time he came near." Atkinson seemed

---

169 Harrison, Scott . "From the Archives: 1940 Opening of the Hollywood Palladium." *Los Angeles Times*, March 16, 2017.

170 "U2 October Tour October 2nd Leg: North America 1981-11-28: Hollywood Palladium - Los Angeles, California, USA." U2gigs.Com. https://www.u2gigs.com/show952.html.

171 Rollins, Henry. 1984. *Get in the Van: On the Road with Black Flag*. Paperback.

bewildered by all the fuss. "U2's two albums have sold well but not spectacularly," he wrote, "and the band's music is often (if erroneously) lumped in with British neo-psychedelic outfits like Echo & the Bunnymen. So why the wild crowd reaction?"

He concluded with an answer to his own question. "U2's music has some dark, swirling qualities and there's plenty of adolescent confusion and anger in the lyrics, but the emphasis is on the celebration of life," he wrote. "It was easy to understand why the crowd almost got carried away."[172]

The Los Angeles Memorial Coliseum

Once known as "The Greatest Stadium in the World," the Coliseum was commissioned in 1921 as a memorial to Los Angeles veterans of World War I. More than a century later, it will become the first stadium to have hosted the Summer Olympics three times in 2028.[173]

U2 connected with the Coliseum on November 17–18, 1987 on the third leg of *The Joshua Tree* tour. The shows are documented as the second go of the infamous prank wherein U2 covertly opened for themselves while playing the members of a fictional band of country music siblings called the Dalton Brothers. As they had done in Indianapolis two weeks prior when scheduled opener Los Lobos was delayed at the airport, U2 took to the stage during the first supporting act slot to perform the twangy "Lucille" (written by Bono) and the 1948 Leon Payne song "Lost Highway." Each band member was dressed in costume to portray an alter ego: "Alton Dalton," (Bono), "Luke Dalton" (Edge), "Duke Dalton" (Larry), and "sister" of the group "Betty Dalton" (Adam).

The *LA Times* write-up days later said, "Many of the estimated 65,000 fans who saw U2's concert Wednesday night at the Los Angeles Memorial Coliseum may still be wondering about those mysterious Dalton Brothers, who performed unannounced, prior to a set by the Pretenders. The shaggy looking country music outfit called itself 'a band from Galveston, Texas that has been a big influence on both U2 and the Pretenders.' Turned out to be the four

---

172 Atkinson, Terry. "U2 Celebrated at the Palladium." *Los Angeles Times*, December 1, 1981.

173 "Coliseum History." Www.Lacoliseum.Com. Los Angeles Coliseum, https://www.lacoliseum.com/coliseum-history/.

members of U2 themselves wearing fake wigs and cowboy hats, and, in one case, a mini-skirt … Only fans seated closest to the stage—or hardcore U2 followers—probably realized that their heroes were on stage."[174] It was U2's only time performing at the Coliseum, but an unforgettable one.

Dodger Stadium

By the time U2 made it to Dodger Stadium in October 1992, *ZooTV* was on its third leg (the stadium iteration of the tour known as "Outdoor Broadcast"). Although they had played the Los Angeles Sports Arena on the first (indoor) leg, the two back-to-back nights outdoors on October 30 and 31 (Halloween weekend 1992) were primed for a more indelible impact.

More than a decade after covering U2's California debut at the Country Club in Reseda, *Los Angeles Times* critic Robert Hilburn also covered the band's first and only stop at Dodger Stadium. The review began, "On a field where the Dodgers recently completed one of the worst seasons in the team's history, U2 brought some thrills back to Dodger Stadium with a pair of masterful weekend concerts."

But when it came to the extravagant *ZooTV* setup, Hilburn took a more critical tone. "Indeed, some of U2's most powerful moments Friday and Saturday came when the video screens were either turned off or greatly downplayed," he wrote. He also referred to Bono's new The Fly persona as "the most unsettling" of all the Halloween costumes present in the stadium that night.[175] At that point, it had been just shy of one year since the world first saw The Fly's debut in the video for the *Achtung Baby* song of the same name (a moment burned in the brains of U2's followers as the manifestation of Bono's promise in the final moments of the 80s to "go away and dream it all up again").[176]

Three decades later, Bono would adopt The Fly character once again for a historic Las Vegas residency that celebrated thirty years

---

174 *"LA Times Morning Report,* Pop/Rock,.", November 20, 1987.

175 Hilburn, Robert . "U2: Power and Thrills." *Los Angeles Times,* November 2, 1992.

176 "U2: Dream It All Up Again Speech." ChillyPhilly. August 24, 2011.
    Video, https://www.youtube.com/watch?v=JkC4ncOqa1w&list=RDJkC4ncOqa1w&start_radio=1.

of *Achtung Baby*. From the Viking 1973 glasses and costuming to the mannerisms and stage gimmicks—brought to life by a much older Bono, then in his 60s—fans devoured all aspects of The Fly's return with palpable enthusiasm.[177] What Hilburn saw as "unsettling" in 1992 would go on to be revered and celebrated by U2's core audience. Some critiques don't stand the test of time, and this was one of them. Perhaps, eventually, that will prove to be the case for other critically unpopular moments in U2 history, such as the move to release *Songs of Innocence* for free on Apple devices in 2014 (a debacle that, as of 2025, continues to produce complaints from its vocal opponents). Time will tell.

The Forum

Also known as the Kia Forum, the Los Angeles Forum, the Inglewood Forum, and (formerly) the Great Western Forum, the international style structure at 3900 West Manchester Boulevard was once one of the best-known indoor sports venues in the U.S. As a music venue, the first artist to play on a Forum stage was Aretha Franklin in January 1968, followed later that year by Santana, Cream, Joan Baez, and The Doors.[178] U2 would first make their way to the Forum in June 1986 for the Conspiracy of Hope benefit show; their next Forum booking was almost thirty years later in November 2015, when they were announced as the night two headliner of another charity show, KROQ's Almost Acoustic Christmas. That same week, Bono suffered devastating injuries in a bicycling accident in New York City's Central Park, forcing the band to back out of the show.[179] It would be five months until they returned to the Forum, but the comeback was a victorious five-night mini-residency for the *Innocence + Experience* tour. It was an eventful week for multiple reasons, including the passing of tour manager Dennis Sheehan at Sunset Marquis in the hours after the first show concluded.

---

177 "U2 UV THE FLY SUNGLASSES." Shop.U2.Com. https://shop.u2.com/products/the-fly-sunglasses?srsltid =AfmBOoqi14ITvR9NxTs4IM1cKJF0ATjx_e-oIATpHf17IB1oFT3FoyNs.

178 "Past The Forum Concerts." ConcertArchives.Com. https://www.concertarchives.org/venues/the-forum.

179 Larsen, Peter. "U2 Is Out, No Doubt Is in for the Second Night of KROQ'S Almost Acoustic Christmas." *Orange County Register*, December 4, 2014.

Among U2's fan base, the *I+E* tour is perhaps best remembered as the last era of accessibility, when fans were given more up-close opportunities with the band than they would be in the years that followed. One reason was more frequent "pulling" of fans onstage than in other tours, thanks to U2's partnership with the live video streaming app Meerkat.[180] The chosen fans would be asked to hold a phone handed to them by either Bono or a stagehand, then film the band for the duration of a song.

Often, this moment occurred during "Mysterious Ways" or "Desire"—but on May 26 at the Forum, it took place during "Sweetest Thing." The lucky fan chosen was Joe Hier, frontman of the renowned U2 tribute Hollywood U2. "You're looking really good, man," Bono told him after asking him to come to the stage.

"I love your early work."[181]

Bono watched, seemingly in amazement,

Photo courtesy of Loli Hier

as Hier sang the first verse of "Sweetest Thing" alongside him with effortless professionalism—and then, he confidently handed over the mic. The rest is U2 history; the story made *Rolling Stone* the next day.[182]

As a staff writer for the website U2 Zoo Station Radio at the time, the author of this book asked Hier, also a personal friend, for a comment on the experience. He replied with a laugh, "I was beside myself."[183]

180 "Innocence + Experience Tour 2015." U2.com. July 14, 2015. https://www.u2.com/tour/date/45561340.

181 "U2 - Sweetest Thing (W/Joseph Hier Hollywood U2) (The Forum, Los Angeles CA 5/26/15)." Brian James. May 27, 2015. Video, https://www.youtube.com/watch?v=nIDSXTSJHyk.

182 Grow, Kory. "Watch U2 Perform 'Sweetest Thing' With Bono Impersonator." Rolling Stone, May 27, 2015. https://www.rollingstone.com/music/music-news/watch-u2-perform-sweetest-thing-with-bono-impersonator-178405/.

183 Flagg, Brook. "U2 Inglewood Forum May 26 Review." U2 Zoo Station Radio. May 27, 2015. https://www.u2radio.com/2015/05/u2-inglewood-forum-may-26th-review/.

The Rose Bowl

When the suggestively space-themed *U2 360° Tour* touched down at Pasadena's Rose Bowl on October 25, 2009, U2 would play to their largest American audience ever: a sold-out crowd of 97,014 people. This broke the previous U.S. record for single concert attendance for a headline act (remarkably, a record *also* held by U2—twice). *Billboard* documented the feat as follows:

It took 22 years, but U2 has broken its own attendance record for the best-attended single concert performance at a U.S. venue by one headliner.

The band's 360 Tour played the Pasadena, Calif. Rose Bowl on Oct. 25 to a sellout crowd of 97,014 — the highest attendance on record for one U.S. show by a single headliner based on box office totals reported to Billboard.

The old record was set on Sept. 25, 1987 at the now-demolished John F. Kennedy Stadium in Philadelphia with a crowd of 86,145 in attendance for the band's Joshua Tree Tour ... Among the top five single-concert attendances on record in the U.S., the top three are all U2 performances. The third-highest attendance is also from the band's current tour at its Sept. 29 sellout at the FedExField in Landover, Md with 84,754.

The attendance record was not the only feat achieved at the Rose Bowl in 2009. *Billboard* also noted record ticket sales:

U2's Rose Bowl show excelled in gross ticket sales as well as attendance. With $9.96 million grossed, it is the second highest-grossing single U.S. concert by a solo headliner. The concert is second only to the Three Tenors' July 20, 1996 sold-out show at Giants Stadium in East Rutherford, N.J.[184]

And finally, a third history-making endeavor: the first time a concert was streamed live on YouTube. It may seem commonplace now, but in 2009, it had never been done before. U2 reached a global audience of 10 million viewers streaming *U2 360°* at the Rose Bowl in real time—once again demonstrating their commitment to pushing boundaries and achieving "intimacy on a grand scale."

---

184 Allen, B. (2009, October 30). U2's Rose Bowl show breaks U.S. Attendance record. Reuters. https://www.reuters.com/article/lifestyle/u2s-rose-bowl-show-breaks-us-attendance-record-idUSTRE59U09W/

A YouTube blog post dated October 19, 2009 teased the live-stream event as follows:

If you are a fan of the Irish rock band U2, you may have already caught wind of a little secret. Earlier today, the band alerted fans that they will be able to watch their upcoming performance from the Rose Bowl in L.A. on their YouTube channel.

If you live in one of the 16 countries listed below*, you can join U2 live on Sunday, October 25 at 8:30 p.m. (PT). In addition with pumping your fist along with Bono, you'll be able to join YouTube's global listening party via a Twitter gadget embedded on U2's YouTube channel. And if you miss the concert, just press play when you wake up or get to a computer: the uploaded rebroadcast of the full show will be available the next day.[185]

As of 2025, this entry still lives on YouTube's News and Events blog.

The band would return to the Rose Bowl six years later for two nights of *The Joshua Tree 2017* tour on May 20 and 21. During night two, Bono dedicated the show to Guus Van Hove and Helena Nuellett, who tragically died in August 2011 while searching for the sacred site of the fallen Joshua tree in the wrong stretch of the Mojave Desert (see Section II). The band also paid tribute to the memory of Chris Cornell, who had passed on May 18, by playing Soundgarden's "Black Hole Sun" before taking the stage.

This time, the *LA Times* review was written by the paper's recently appointed pop music critic Mikael Wood. After a thorough breakdown of the show's three-act progression (three to four early U2 songs; all eleven songs of *The Joshua Tree* in original sequence; six to seven additional songs from other U2 eras), Wood concluded his review with the provocative question, "If Saturday's gig made 1987 come alive, it also made you wonder: What will U2 be reviving in 2047?"[186]

Time will tell whether U2 is still performing in 2047, seventy-one years after forming the band. We should be so lucky.

---

185 Flannery, Michelle . "U2 on YouTube -- Live!" Blog.Youtube.Com. October 19, 2009. https://blog.youtube/news-and-events/u2-on-youtube-live/.

186 Wood, Mikael. "What Worked and what Didn't at U2's 'The Joshua Tree' Revival at the Rose Bowl." *Los Angeles Times*, May 21, 2017.

The Joshua Tree 2017 stage, Rose Bowl
Photo by Brook W. Flagg

The Forum, 2015

Adam photo by Chris Phillips

Edge, Larry, and Bono photos by Christopher Flagg

SECTION VI

Zuma Beach

The Sacred Site
of the Coast

Zuma Beach: The Sacred Site of the Coast

Location: Point Dume Beach Lot, 7103 Westward Beach Road, Malibu

Sacredness: Integral to U2's arrival in California; enigmatic song inspiration; multiple full band visits over 40 years; *SOI + SOE* album recording; a mysteriously disappearing video shoot

Dates in U2 history: Various, 1981-2017

Still in operation/visitable? Yes

"It's funny how songs, you don't really know what you're writing about half the time, and this song was set out there on Zuma Beach."
— Bono, live at the Roxy Theatre, May 28, 2015

The "California" Connection

At first glance, the connection between U2 and Zuma Beach is as appropriately opaque as the salty Pacific—and yet, its sugary sands contain a treasure trove of U2 mythos which is yet to be fully uncovered.

It was not until *Songs of Innocence (SOI)* was released in 2014 that Zuma Beach was mentioned in U2 lyrics, as the backdrop of the song "California (There is No End to Love)."

California

Then we fell into the shiny sea

The weight that drags your heart down

Well that's what took me

Where I need to be

Which is here, out on Zuma

Watching you cry like a baby

California, at the dawn

You thought would never come

But it did, like it always does

Despite its depiction of an emotional, cathartic experience "out on Zuma," the song is often recognized for its earlier reference to a different coastal city. In the Beach Boys-inspired introduction, the first vocals on "California" come from Edge (now well-known as a resident of Malibu since the early 2000s). As the song opens, Edge softly repeats, "Ba-Ba-Barbara, Santa Barbara" as the accompaniment swells like the surf at high tide. Of course, Zuma Beach and Santa Barbara are separated by sixty-five miles. But maybe that's the point; California is vast, and its coastline diverse.

Zuma in Early U2 Lore

In a piece published on September 9, 2014—the day of *SOI's* release—Bono said of the song to *Rolling Stone*, "It's like the sun itself. It's about our first trip to Los Angeles."[187] One week later, he repeated the claim when speaking with Irish radio journalist Dave Fanning: "'California' is about our first time of going to Los Angeles, and California and all of that."[188]

As written in Section I, the band's first visit to Los Angeles was during the *Boy* tour to play the Reseda Country Club on March 15, 1981. Is it possible that a trip to Zuma was also on the itinerary that week—perhaps on March 14 or 17 (the only dates that week with no shows booked)? If what Bono shared at U2's intimate Roxy Theatre performance in West Hollywood on May 28, 2015 is to be believed, then the answer is yes.

"It's funny how songs, you don't really know what you're writing about half the time, and this song was set out there on Zuma Beach," he said. "We had arrived on our very first tour ... We went out to try and find Brian Wilson's house, because we'd heard he had a piano and a sand pit—and we just thought this man had the music of the spheres, you know? He was incredible.

"We had a copy of the Beach Boys at our very first rehearsal," he continued. "... And this, of course, doesn't sound anything like the Beach Boys, but it's another song—as they all seem to be—

---

187 Wenner, Gus. "Exclusive: Bono Reveals Secrets of U2'S Surprise Album 'Songs of Innocence.'" *Rolling Stone*, September 9, 2014. https://www.rollingstone.com/music/music-news/exclusive-bono-reveals-secrets-of-u2s-surprise-album-songs-of-innocence-106257/.

188 Dave Fanning Interviews Bono on New U2 Album Songs of Innocence." RTE, September 21, 2014. https://www.rte.ie/radio/2fm/clips/20652051/.

about grief, and the defiance that is the joy of rock and roll. This is 'California.'"[189]

Among the many dozen promotional appearances and interviews surrounding *SOI* and the *I+E* tour throughout 2014 and 2015, this may be the only time any member of U2 has told this story to an audience—and with that, the significance of Zuma Beach in U2 history was substantially deepened.

The Zuma Timeline

No End to Grief (1981)

The Santa Barbara Mission bells are faintly heard as "California" begins, but Zuma is namechecked one minute and ten seconds into the song as Bono sings about "watching you cry like a baby," both on the beach and in a bedroom mirror. Later in the song, a refrain he would repeat over the next several years—both from the stage and in his *Surrender* memoir—delivers the song's strongest punch: "There's no end to grief. That's how I know, and why I need to know that there is no end to love."[190] When Bono speaks on grief, it's often in reference to the lasting effects of losing his mother, Iris Hewson, at age 14—or the loss of U2 assistant Greg Carroll, whose death in 1986 inspired "One Tree Hill" for *The Joshua Tree*. But in "California," it seems the bereaved party who wept on Zuma is not Bono until the second verse, when the pronoun switches to "yourself." In the first verse, we aren't meant to know *who* "you" is, or when their grief began. It may be one of the other band members; it may not. The ambiguity of the lyric is textbook Bono songwriting: specific to the band, but applicable to anyone.

Despite the grief enigma presented in the "California" lyrics, Bono's remarks at the Roxy uncovered at least one part of the story on how Zuma inspired the band, placing the event of their first visit firmly in March 1981. Unfortunately, there are no published photos of U2's first trip to Zuma—just a story and a song.

189 U2 West Hollywood Roxy Theatre California." Lorna Cairns. May 28, 2015. Video, https://www.youtube.com/watch?v=F29CES6_4mA.

190 Bono. 2022. *Surrender: 40 Songs, One Story*. Penguin Random House.

Shooting at Point Dume (1985)

The next time U2 would visit Zuma—and the band's first documented photo shoot on the beach—took place almost exactly four years later. Photographer Neal Preston, who graciously granted an interview for this book in October 2025, recalled that he shot the band on assignment for *People* magazine.

Preston—renowned for his work with Led Zeppelin, Queen, The Who, and Bruce Springsteen among many others as documented in his 2017 book *Exhilarated and Exhausted*—worked with U2 a handful of times over the decades due to a long-term contract with Time-Life, Inc. The most notable of those assignments: shooting the band backstage at Arizona State University during the first *The Joshua Tree* tour dates for their iconic *Time* cover story, "Rock's Hottest Ticket," in April '87. When running into Bono at a later date, Preston would say, "Bono, that was my first *Time* cover!" The singer replied, "Thanks, Neal—it was mine too!"

Two years prior in March '85, Preston captured the band for *People* at the stunning Point Dume promontory at the south end of Zuma. Preston shared that he was tasked with choosing the location because in those days, *People* wanted their story subjects to be photographed at home ("somewhere that would surprise people, somewhere [readers] hadn't seen them before," he recalled)—and in 1985, no one in U2 had a home base in LA. "It was up to me to figure it out," he said. "It's my decision what makes sense for that magazine, given the amount of time that the band does or doesn't have. So I said 'OK, where am I going to shoot these guys?' And I remember saying, 'How about I shoot them at the beach?'" Preston was unaware the band had been to Zuma previously, and was surprised to hear of Bono's 2015 recollections on an emotional day there in 1981.

So why did he choose *that* beach, specifically, over any other stretch of Southern California coastline? More than forty years on, it's a grainy memory. "Maybe I had been to Zuma before," he wondered, "or maybe I just said, 'it's a really nice day.' But I do remember it was a fucking long drive, and I thought they didn't know that. But I guess they *did* know."

It was the fifth leg of *The Unforgettable Fire* tour, and the band was in town to play the Sports Arena for three dates: March 2, 4 and 5. When asked if that meant his shoot with the band in Zuma took place on March 3, Preston replied, "You probably know better than I do!"

Preston's Point Dume photos depict a somber U2, all four dressed in wildly inappropriate clothing for their surroundings. The look is characteristic of *The Unforgettable Fire* era: all black, long sleeves, giant hats, restrained smiles.

"They were as I expected them to be," Preston said. "They weren't like the Monkees, but they weren't like the Sex Pistols either. They knew 'This is part of what we have to do.' It was business as usual. And they were nice enough."

Preston's characteristically sardonic delivery is encapsuled in his remarks on the band's solemn attire: "So he wore a hat," he said with a laugh. "Big fucking deal."

Nowadays, Point Dume is a popular spot for engagement photos, amateur drones, and Instagram shoots; this ensures an eclectic bunch is likely to populate the spot at any given time. Re-creating one or more of the band's poses for the Preston shoot can be simple for a group of four fans; simply dress in mourner's attire and stand in front of the bluff at Point Dume with each person spaced about two feet apart, keeping facial expressions steady and serious. It's unlikely that anyone will blink twice at an oddly dressed foursome of U2 fans attempting a photo re-creation.

Fan re creation, 2022

Returning to Zuma (2014)

While the Preston shoot was the band's first Zuma visit to be documented in photos, it would not be their last. Another shoot would take place on Zuma Beach almost thirty years later in 2014, in connection with the release of *SOI* (although not at Point Dume). Presumably, the intention was to use footage of the band strolling on the beach for a "California" video—and yet, an official video of this nature never surfaced. The still shots that briefly circulated online were limited to one of the band walking along the ocean with a videographer visible, and one featuring the band in a stationary pose on the ramp of a lifeguard tower. These photos are not known to be connected to any official publication or photographer.

One of the photos contains an additional clue regarding a possible intention for its use. In the background of the lifeguard tower photo is branding for the annual Nautica Malibu Triathlon, which takes place every September (the same month as the SOI release in 2014). This reinforces the idea that the photo was originally intended to promote "California," perhaps as a single. Had SOI not been the target of widespread, media-driven vitriol due to the controversy involving the band's partnership with Apple to distribute the album for free via the iTunes accounts of users, perhaps

U2 would have moved forward with using the Zuma footage for some type of "California" promotion (aside from the animated video created for the "Films of Innocence" release). Instead, only three singles were released from the album as the band shifted its focus to prepare for the Innocence + Experience tour, which launched in May 2015. One of those singles was "Song for Someone," which was released with a video featuring only one band member, Bono. The video was shot by Matt Mahurin with Bono in Malibu (though not explicitly Zuma, to the best of this author's knowledge) on August 27, 2015.[191]

---

191 "U2 Videos - Filming Locations." U2songs.Com. https://www.u2songs.com/maps/videos

Recording at Shangri-La (2017)

SOI was recorded at seven recording studios in the United States and Europe; two of those studios are located in Malibu near Zuma. The first, Woodshed Recording, was narrowly spared from the Woolsey Wildfire of 2018; the residence on the property, owned by studio operators Richard and Linda Gibbs, was not.[192] The second, Shangri-La Studio, is perched on the bluffs directly above Zuma and owned by producer Rick Rubin.[193] In conjunction with the album's unveiling, U2 released a vignette-style video of Bono and Edge working alongside conductor David Campbell at Shangri-La on a string section for a new arrangement of the album's second track, "Every Breaking Wave."[194] The slowed-down arrangement was adapted using a piano on the *I+E* tour the following year, with a similar arrangement featured on the band's *Songs of Surrender* release in 2023. Because of the live performance saturation of these arrangements, they may be more recognizable to fans than the original, up-tempo recording of the song.

With Larry in Zuma (2014)
Courtesy of Charlie Torrealba

For the successor to *SOI*, 2017's *Songs of Experience (SOE)*, U2 returned to Shangri-La to record again. *Q Magazine* met with the band on location to produce an article titled "Hard Won Experience," in which *SOE* is called U2's "political and personal apocalypse."[195] The story features a photo of Bono at the studio in front of Bob Dylan's retired tour bus.

192 Owsinski, Bobby . "Your Studio Might Be Safe From Wildfire, But Not From The Insurance Company." *Forbes*, May 11, 2020. https://www.forbes.com/sites/bobbyowsinski/2020/05/11/your-studio-might-be-safe-from-wildfire-but-not-from-the-insurance-company/

193 DeRiso, Nick. "Key Piece of Rock History Has Somehow Survived the LA Fires." *Ultimate Classic Rock*, January 16, 2025. https://ultimateclassicrock.com/shangri-la-studios-los-angeles-fires/.

194 "'Every Breaking Wave' (Vignette)." U2.Com. February 25, 2015. https://www.u2.com/news/title/studio-exclusive/.

195 Doyle, Tom. "Hard-Won Experience." Q, December 1, 2017.

U2 + Zuma = Elusive + Obvious

The nature of U2's long-term relationship with Zuma Beach is both elusive and obvious. Like the band's pairing of innocence and experience, the connection between four Irish musicians swaddled in heavy black garments and a sun-drenched beach well-known for hosting surf competitions is nearly paradoxical. But that element of mystery— along with the spirituality innate to this stretch of ocean, where dolphin pods and migrating gray whales can be spotted daily— makes the natural wonder of Point Dume at Zuma

Photos by Brook W. Flagg

Beach a must-visit for those sojourning through the sacred U2 sites of Southern California.

October 2022

SECTION VII

Sites of Significance

in Greater Palm Springs

Sites of Significance in Greater Palm Springs

Dominick's restaurant and bar
Location: 70030 CA-111, Rancho Mirage
Significance: "I've Got You Under My Skin" video shoot with Frank Sinatra
Still in operation/visitable? No
Building still standing? Yes (now Enzo's Bistro & Bar)

Las Casuelas Nuevas restaurant
Location: 70050 CA-111, Rancho Mirage
Significance: Dinner with Sinatra; attempt to convince Sinatra to record "One Shot of Happy, Two Shots of Sad"
Still in operation/visitable? Yes, with patronage
Building still standing? Yes (now Enzo's Bistro & Bar)

Significance: Dinner with Frank Sinatra

Still in operation/visitable? Yes, with patronage

While U2's connection to the desert is primarily in the high desert region, the band members have descended on Palm Springs and its surrounding low desert communities several times over the decades. Here are the most notable of those times.

Palm Springs International Film Festival (2014)

On January 4, 2014, Bono and Edge represented U2 at the Palm Springs International Film Festival to collect the Sonny Bono Visionary Award, in connection with the band's contribution to the film *Mandela: Long Walk to Freedom* (the Oscar-nominated song "Ordinary Love"). The two made a splash with a joint speech that was playful on the part of Edge, who had fun with the pronunciation of the phonetically short "o" sound in Bono's name vs. the long "o" in the name of the late musician/Palm Springs mayor Bono, for whom the award was named. As for the "short o Bono," his acceptance remarks to the audience of filmmakers and other artists were characteristically inspirational: "You all know that a vision

without a promise is just a fantasy. And we're not interested in that."
He also delivered the quote that opens this book: "… More people
live off their imaginations in California than any other place in the
world. No other geography comes close."[196]

Friendship/Collaboration with Frank Sinatra (1993)

U2's first well-known connection to Palm Springs is Bono's 1993
collaboration with Frank Sinatra for a cover of Sinatra's tune "I've
Got You Under My Skin," the first single for Sinatra's *Duets* album.
The video is a cornucopia of swanky images related to Sinatra
and Palm Springs, including a cheeky shot of Sonny Bono's Italian
eatery that once sat at the corner of Indian Canyon Drive and East
Via Escuela (Mayor Bono sold the establishment in 1991).[197] These
images alternate with cuts to footage of U2's Bono appearing to
drive himself on Highway 111 toward Palm Springs, as if making a
solo trip to the desert hideaway from Los Angeles. In one brief shot,
we see him breeze eastbound on I-10 past the Cabazon Dinosaurs
freeway attraction. It also features footage of Bono and Sinatra
cruising around the city in a limousine en route to the two Rancho
Mirage restaurants they would visit that day.[198]

"Waiting for an Irish Crooner to Arrive" at Dominick's

Although Rancho Mirage is roughly twenty minutes east of Palm
Springs, it is generally considered one of several nearby cities that
make up the greater Palm Springs area. One of Sinatra's favorite
spots there was Dominick's, which was located at 70030 CA-111
(now occupied by an establishment called Enzo's Bistro and Bar).

In 2015, Bruce Fessier wrote in *The Desert Sun*, "By the 1970s
and 80s, Sinatra's two favorite Rancho Mirage restaurants are
Dominick's and Lord Fletcher's … (Dominick's) becomes Sinatra's
favorite place to watch *Monday Night Football*." It was Fessier who
confirmed Dominick's as the site of the video shoot, writing, "When

196 "U2News - Sonny Bono Visionary Award 2014." Ezequiel EspañOl. January 4, 2014.
    Video, https://www.youtube.com/watch?v=YHitTokwedI.

197 Hubler, Shawn. "Bono Selling His Popular Restaurant, Tennis Club." *Los Angeles Times*, April 14, 1991.

198 "Frank Sinatra & Bono – I've Got You Under My Skin." U2. May 10, 2020.
    Video, https://www.youtube.com/watch?v=pL3ZVzWdaS4&list=RDpL3ZVzWdaS4&start_radio=1.

U2's Bono comes to town to shoot a video of 'I've Got You Under My Skin' from Sinatra's smash 1993 album '*Duets*,' they shoot it at Dominick's."[199]

In his *Surrender* memoir, Bono wrote of the experience, "… We'd met up in the California desert to shoot a video for 'I've Got You Under My Skin.' With the director Kevin Godley and his crew on our tail, we shared a limo ride to a Palm Springs bar, owned by one of Frank's friends. The idea was that Frank and I would shoot the breeze … opening scene was Frank at the bar on his own waiting for an Irish crooner to arrive, which I did for the first time." The scenes are extremely brief, due to what Bono wrote was "some kind of misunderstanding," implied to be connected to the aging Sinatra's short fuse with the film crew.[200]

"Tequila in Fishbowl Glasses" at Las Casuelas Nuevas

Bono and Edge joined Frank and Barbara Sinatra for dinner that night at Las Casuelas Nuevas, next door to Dominick's on Highway 111 (not to be confused with the better-known Las Casuelas location on Palm Canyon Drive in Palm Springs proper).

In Bono's written account of the dinner, he recalls Sinatra holding up a blue napkin and uttering the poignant reflection, "I remember when my eyes were this blue." He also references "drinking tequila in huge fishbowl glasses" and pitching the song "Two Shots of Happy, One Shot of Sad."[201] Sinatra would never record the song (in fact, he would never record another original song in his lifetime). At the *Sinatra 100: An All-Star Grammy Concert*, which aired on CBS in December 2015, Bono introduced the song by saying, "Edge and myself pitched this next song to Frank at a table at a Mexican restaurant in Palm Springs. And then we wondered why he never recorded it."[202]

---

199 Fessier, Bruce. "Dueling Personalities." *Desert Sun*, October 15, 2015.

200 Bono. 2022. *Surrender: 40 Songs, One Story*. Penguin Random House.

201 Ibid.

202 "U2 - Two Shots Of Happy, One Shot Of Sad - Live From London, 2 November 2015." Beautiful Ghost. December 17, 2020. Video, https://www.youtube.com/watch?v=Vfh9IC8jnJA&list=RDVfh9IC8jnJA&start_radio=1.

at a Mexican restaurant in

EXIT 112

111

Palm Springs

One shot
of happy

OPEN SUNDAY at 10:30am

Las Casuelas Nuevas
RESTAURANTE Y CANTINA

Two shots of
sad

The Blue
Napkin

I've got you
under my skin

Bono has never included the name of the restaurant in his accounts. Fortunately, the reporter Fessier documented it. "Bono recalled visiting a Mexican restaurant," Fessier wrote for *The Desert Sun* in 2014, "which Mary Bono and I reminded him was Las Casuelas Nuevas."[203]

The Sinatra Residence

"Edge and I had spent some time at [Sinatra's] house in Palm Springs, looking out onto the desert and hills, no gingham for miles."
                              – Bono, *Surrender: 40 Songs, One Story*, 2022

In his *Surrender* memoir, Bono continued to describe his evening at the Sinatra home (although not confirmed, this may have been Sinatra's Rancho Mirage home as opposed to his Villa Maggio estate overlooking Palm Desert or his Twin Palms home in Palm Springs proper).

There, Bono wrote, he experienced the embarrassment of thinking he had wet himself, only to discover he had simply spilled his drink while nodding off. "I guess I was drunk," he wrote, "high on Frank, a shrinking shadowboxing short-ass following in this giant's footsteps ... We went back to the hotel. Turn left on Frank Sinatra Drive. I knew I would never drink in the company of this great man again."[204]

203 Fessier, Bruce. "Frank Sinatra Hoopla Eclipses Lennon, Elvis and Billie." *Desert Sun*, December 8, 2015.

204 Bono. 2022. *Surrender: 40 Songs, One Story*. Penguin Random House.

Photo by Brook W. Flagg

SECTION VIII

Sites of Significance
in
San Diego

Sites of Significance in San Diego

US Grant Hotel

Location: 326 Broadway, San Diego, CA 92101

Significance: Band antics with fans from hotel balcony on *The Joshua Tree* tour

Still in operation/visitable? Yes, with patronage

Horton Plaza Fountain/Broadway Fountain

Location: 397 Broadway, San Diego, CA 92101

Significance: Bono joins fans at fountain on *The Joshua Tree* tour

Still in operation/visitable? Not in operation, with limited access (surrounded by a barrier)

Still standing? Yes

The U2 presence in San Diego may be minimal compared to other Southern California regions, but its place in the band's history is nonetheless unique.

It starts with a bit of intrigue rooted in the *Boy* tour—a mystery that hinges on the answer to a decades-old question:

Was there a U2 show in San Diego on March 13, 1981?
The general consensus is an emphatic *no*. However, the rumor that such a show happened has repeatedly resurfaced over the decades.

   Does it matter? For the purposes of accurately cataloging U2 tour history, yes. If the rumor was true, then San Diego would be the site of U2's first California performance—not, as most authoritative sources contend, the Country Club in Reseda.
This book takes the position that the San Diego rumor is not true. But where did it originate, and why does it persist to this day?

The San Diego Rumor: What We Know

The conventional belief is that the first U2 concert in California took place on March 15, 1981 at the Country Club in Reseda. The mystique surrounding a rumored San Diego show before it (on either March 13 or 14) casts the only remaining doubt. Some have claimed this show happened at a now-closed bar on the University of California San Diego campus called the Backdoor Café; others have said the band played at the Old Globe Theatre on one of those two nights. Some fan-managed concert archives have logged these possibilities in their databases, as does the print book *U2 Live: A Concert Documentary* by the late Primm Jal de la Parra.[205]

An entry for the date on U2songs.com states in part, "Over the years a couple of locations have been suggested, including the Old Globe Theatre, however The Old Globe Theatre was consumed in a fire on March 8, 1978. The entire theatre had been destroyed in minutes. And it did not reopen until 1982. The Backdoor Café at San Diego State University has also been suggested, but the talent booker for that venue in 1982 had passed on U2, saying they wanted too much money. He told *The Union Tribune* that he 'didn't think more than five people would come.'"[206]

"Among the Most Puzzling in U2 History"

Broadly, most authoritative sources on live U2 history concede that a San Diego show ultimately did *not* take place on the *Boy* tour. But what accounts for the confusion?

A lengthy elucidation on U2gigs.com states in part, "The circumstances of this concert (including whether it even happened) are among the most puzzling in U2's history ... It is likely that a date of 14 March was originally scheduled, but after the initial radio promotions, the concert had to be rescheduled to a day earlier for unknown reasons ... Whoever was in charge of booking locations

---

205 De la Parra, Pimm Jal. 1994. *U2 Live: A Concert Documentary.* Omnibus Pr & Schirmer Trade Books.

206 "1981-03-14 The Old Globe Theatre, San Diego, California." U2songs.Com. https://www.u2songs.com/shows/1981_03_14_u2_the_old_globe_theatre_san_diego_california.

was confident enough to list the Backdoor in ads, but this fell through during negotiations over the fee."[207]

All things considered, it's entirely possible that U2's California inception was *almost* in the coastal urbania of San Diego—but in the end, it most certainly was not. Still, the suggestion that a San Diego show preceded Reseda plays a curious role in early U2 lore.

A Historic Hotel & "Lucille" at the Fountain

The next time San Diego would play a key role in U2 history was April 14, 1987, when *The Joshua Tree* tour stopped for two nights at the San Diego Sports Arena. Due to demand created by the band skipping San Diego on *The Unforgettable Fire* tour, the ticket sale set a record for the venue by selling out in one hour and seventeen minutes, an impressive feat by 1980s standards. The night two show marked the first time "Mothers of the Disappeared" was played; over the next thirty-two years, it would be played a total of eighty-nine times. But it's what happened *after* the two nights of shows concluded that makes the U.S. Grant Hotel and adjacent Horton Park Plaza Fountain, also known as the Broadway Fountain, a combined site of significance in San Diego.

The episode involves some late-night antics between the band and a group of fans who gathered to greet them outside the hotel—a true "stuff of legend" sequence of events that can't be replicated today. The book *U2 Live: A Concert Documentary* told the story this way:

"After the show, a group of around forty fans wait for U2 at the entrance to their hotel, and are delighted when they spend time talking and signing autographs. Offered an acoustic guitar, Bono plays a quick version of 'Lucille,' the recently written country song also performed in Tuscon, before he went up to his room. The fans serenade the band with U2 songs from across the street. Edge appears on the balcony, chants with the fans, then gets a flashlight to introduce Adam and Larry, illuminating their faces. Larry gives a one-man show, taking off his shirt, flexing his muscles, then dropping his pants to flash his bare bottom to the crowd below. Later, Bono comes down to join the fans and sits on the edge of a fountain in the little park in front of the hotel.

207 "U2 Boy Tour Boy 4th Leg: North America 1981-03-13: Backdoor - San Diego, California, USA." U2gigs.Com. https://www.u2gigs.com/show164.html.

Fans gather around and again somebody hands him a guitar to sing 'Lucille,' followed by 'Knocking On Heaven's Door' and 'I Still Haven't Found.'"[208]

One of the assembled fans, Ryan Carroll, shared his reflections. "We got word of where they were staying and went directly after night two," he said. "It's a pretty historical hotel here in San Diego, the U.S. Grant. Across the street is the Horton Plaza Fountain, where we gathered. As we waited for any of the four to come down for a meet and greet, Larry mooned us from his window! He just dropped his trousers and put his ass out the window."

Carroll continued, "Ten minutes later, here comes Bono out of the lobby, acoustic guitar in his hand. He walks across the street to the fountain. It's like 2:00 a.m. and he plays 'Knocking on Heaven's Door' and 'Lucille.' And nobody got that but us. I wish we had a cell phone at the time; all we can do now is talk about it."

It's a moment that could only exist in the pre-smartphone era, and it happened at a historic San Diego hotel that has, to date, welcomed twelve U.S. presidents.

Subsequent Stops in San Diego

U2 continued to stop in San Diego intermittently over the decades, starting with the first and third legs of *ZooTV*, followed by a single *Popmart* tour show on April 28, 1997 (this author's first U2 concert), and a single *Elevation* tour date in 2001.

U-2 SAN DIEGO
Advance Tickets
(619) 581-1000 Ticket price
Includes service charge.

---

208 De la Parra, Pimm Jal. 1994. *U2 Live: A Concert Documentary.* Omnibus Pr & Schirmer Trade Books.

In 2005, San Diego would make more U2 history by kicking off the *Vertigo* tour—but from there, the band would skip over the city for the next two tours.

The next time U2 played San Diego would be *The Joshua Tree 2017* at SDCCU Stadium (pictured in the title image of this section). During this final stop in the States before the tour moved into Mexico and South America, Bono made multiple references to "the 619," the predominant area code for San Diego County.[209]

The totality of these offbeat events (and rumors thereof) make for a quirky, curious connection between U2 and this southernmost California city.

---

209 "Opening Set LIVE U2 9-22-17 Qualcomm Stadium, San Diego, CA." Cool Hand 62. September 23, 2017. Video, https://www.youtube.com/watch?v=oOdsqC4ljis.

THE
US GRANT

The Larry balcony

June 2025

Vent to Broadway Fountain...

...Sadly, no longer operatin

Bono w/ fans at the fountain April 1987

Acknowledgements

Remarkably, there are no published U2 lyrics that include the words "grateful" or "gratitude." In the absence of an appropriate lyric to quote, I wish to thank a number of people who encouraged, inspired, or assisted the creation of this book.

First and foremost, thank you to the "U2 sisters" who have shared with me many (if not most) of the journeys to these sites. In alphabetical order: Novelle Best, Soledad Rojas Guitierrez, Noemi Kuznicki, Estela Toledo, Kathrin Van Gilder, Joanne Vega, Wendy Ufford. Every trip is touched by a little bit of magic, even when there's an equal amount of chaos. To others who have joined along the way, I'm grateful for my times with you as well.

Thank you to the 250+ and counting members of U2 Fans of SoCal, my little Facebook community that could. We are ten years in now—so as someone we love has been known to say, "Thanks for sticking around."

Thank you to the passionate U2 tribute community in Southern California, most notably those affiliated with Hollywood U2: Joe Hier, Loli Hier, Stevie Adams, Chas Alm, Steve Judd, and Michael Rostovos.

Thank you to the proprietors of U2 Zoo Station Radio (U2Radio. com), Kevin Dolph and Joshua Eubanks. You gave me my first opportunity to write about the band many years ago, and I remain thankful for it as well as for your ongoing support. Thank you to Joe Pitella, who introduced us.

Many thanks are due to Bill See and Courtney Lavender, who graciously took on beta reading roles for this book and provided their knowledgeable feedback, which was happily incorporated. Courtney, thank you for your beautiful photos of the Roxy and allowing me to collage them haphazardly. Bill, thank you for contributing your wonderful essay on page 140—and another thanks to you and Melody Muraca for weaving the narrative of the *War* tour trifecta described in Section I. Thank you to Corey Lesh for sharing the literature for A Celebration from your archives.

Thank you to the great rock photographer Neal Preston. You are my first midnight interview and I'll never forget it. Thank you for the generosity that enabled me to feature two of your 1985 *People* magazine photos of U2 at Zuma Beach.

Thank you to another outstanding photographer, Kevin Estrada, whose 1983 LA Sports Arena photo is featured on page 7.

Thank you to those who contributed photos of their own trips to The Sacred Sites of *The Joshua Tree*: Colleen Grattan, Kevin Shannon, Anna Conway, Courtney Lavender, Lisa Sloan, Rhonda Sayers Wood, Monica Moser, Christine Spencer, Amanda Zimmerman, Mike Kurman, Steve Follman, and Chris Phillips. Thank you to the fan-managed resources that are quoted here for informational and educational purposes: U2gigs.com, U2tours.com, U2songs.com, the *U2-Y* podcast, and the *Into the Heart of U2* podcast.

Thank you to Edward Platero and George for sharing their deep knowledge and passion for the sacred tree site. I truly hope your vision for its long-term preservation comes to pass, and I encourage other fans to embrace that vision as well so that it will continue to be a destination sought by fans from around the world.

Thank you to everyone who is featured in my photographs. You are all beautiful humans who look fantastic. I regret that there is not enough space to name everyone, but I hope that every featured person feels special.

Thank you to the fans who are quoted, and/or submitted other contextual contributions: Ryan Carroll, Simone Trimm, Scott Middleman, Jeff Fairbanks, Rhonda Sayers-Wood, Courtney Lavender, Mike Muckenthaler, Dave Burton, Ken Wong, Jan Sandys-Renton, Jeanette Narciso, and Charlie Torrealba.

There may be some whose contributions were not included, and I extend sincerest apologies for that. This book was created over more than two years of ups and downs.

Thank you to the dear friends who are *not* U2 friends, most notably Elissa and Richie. Sedona is a whole other type of sacred site, as we know.

Thank you to the professionals who have guided and supported my personal development. Although names are not appropriate, I am very grateful for your patience and assistance.

Thank you to my loving and supportive family: Chris, Felicity, Serenity, Mom and Keith, Cherry and Harry.

This book begins with a grateful dedication and ends with an equally grateful acknowledgement to U2, the greatest living band on the planet. The end is not coming ... and I'll leave it at that.

Brook W. Flagg
November 2025

About the Author

Brook W. Flagg is a writer and editor from Southern California who has worked in various communications roles since 2006. Although she has previously ghostwritten titles for other authors, *I Go There With You* is her first book. She has been a staff writer at U2Radio.com since 2014, and the founder/administrator of the U2 Fans of SoCal Facebook community since 2016. Follow on IG @BrookWF and X @U2RadioBrook; contact via brookwf@gmail.com.